# M I

*of*

# PIERREPONT

## JILL SOUTHERN-JONES

*with* KATHLEEN McANEAR SMITH

Sovereign World

Published by Sovereign World Ltd
PO Box 784
Ellel
Lancaster
LA1 9DA
United Kingdom

Published in 2015

www.sovereignworld.com
Twitter: @sovereignworld
Facebook: www.facebook.com/sovereignworld

ISBN: 9781852407407

Cover illustration by James Hodges
Book production by Zaccmedia (www.zaccmedia.com)
Printed in the United Kingdom

# A Word of Thanks

To every member of the Pierrepont team, past and present, including volunteers, I want to thank you from the bottom of my heart. None of this could have happened without you. You have given your time, your resources, your support, your friendship, your heart and soul to God's work at Pierrepont and I am so deeply grateful to every one of you.

I also want to thank Peter and Fiona Horrobin who have supported me, encouraged me, envisioned me, taught me and believed in me since the beginning. Peter leads Ellel Ministries with enormous vision, wisdom and grace. He is an extraordinary leader whose humble, gentle spirit, obedience to God, perseverance and anointed, biblical teaching are an inspiration to all of us.

And a special thank you to Kathleen McAnear Smith, who was the inspiration behind this book and has put countless hours into it. Kathleen is a beautiful person and a good friend. Her creativity, fantastic writing skills, perseverance and patience are the reason this story has made it into print. Thank you!

And thanks above all to God our Father and to the Lord Jesus Christ. Who You are, and what You have done just humbles and amazes me beyond words.

*Jill Southern-Jones*
*January 2015*

# Contents

# Foreword

*by Peter Horrobin*

It was three o'clock in the morning, following an eventful night during the summer of 1992. A team of us had been ministering late into the night to a lady who had suffered terrible things during her upbringing. She was very fragile and very hurting and we were learning how to apply some of the wonderful keys to healing that are in God's Word.

As we prayed with her, we saw some amazing breakthroughs in the story of her healing and restoration. But the ministry team were exhausted. And that night, as I collapsed into bed, I was crying out to God for His answers for the many thousands more people who also needed such help. The essence of my prayer was, "Lord, how can we answer the cries of so many with so few resources?"

As I slipped into that semi-conscious pre-sleep period before exhaustion takes over, I suddenly became aware of the Lord speaking to me. I knew it was Him, for it was just the same voice that I had heard when God called me into the ministry many years earlier. And it was the same voice which had witnessed into my spirit that Ellel Grange, in the northwest of England, was the place where the work would begin. This time I could only sense the Lord saying to me two words: "Teaching hospital".

I knew instantly what that meant. Both my brother and my daughter were doctors and a key part of their training had been to learn on the job, with real live patients, under the tutelage of experienced consultants in a medical teaching hospital. In spite of my exhaustion, I was now wide awake and working out in my mind the ramifications of what it would mean for Ellel Ministries to establish a new centre, which would be set up along the lines of a spiritual teaching hospital, where many people could learn on the job, with experienced team members to teach them.

As I thought through the consequences of what I believed God had said, the vision for what would become the NETS programme at Ellel Pierrepont was conceived, even though it would be another two years before I would know that Pierrepont itself even existed, and it would be a further two years before Andy Taylor would coin the name NETS, embracing the special verse of Scripture that the Lord had given me for the ministry many years previously. And so it was that the (Luke) Nine Eleven Training School was birthed in the spirit, long before it would become a physical reality.

I eventually fell asleep, but when I woke the following morning, the vision was still there. When I then shared this further development of the vision for Ellel Ministries with the rest of the leadership team at Ellel Grange, they weren't, however, terribly excited at first. The whole team was already running at the limit of their capacity and the idea of adding a third centre in the UK, following so quickly on the heels of the second centre, Glyndley Manor, filled them more with apprehension than with joy.

I totally understood their reaction. We were all struggling with the pressures, but in my mind I was already thinking about where the 'teaching hospital' could be established. For in my spirit, it already existed. This was how God had worked with me when looking for Ellel Grange and I had no reason to question that God would eventually show us where the 'teaching hospital' would be. There was absolutely no doubt in my mind that this was needed to multiply the effectiveness of the ministry, in teaching and training people from all over the world in how to bring hope and healing to the hurting.

And so the search began for a suitable location. There was no immediate answer to our prayers, but during the months of waiting for God to show His hand, the whole vision for the work of the new centre grew and developed, so that when, eventually, God put His finger on Pierrepont as the location for the work, much had already been done in thinking through how the operation could be carried out.

For many months I scoured the advertisements of property agents all over the country. We went as a team to look at a former school that seemed very suitable, but it was sold before we got a chance to make an offer. There were times of doubt as big question marks hung over the vision. But I was sure in my heart that it was from the Lord and that He would show the way.

One very important lesson I had learned on the journey so far was never to divert from what God had already given me to do, no matter how interesting or attractive the diversion might seem. So, even though the idea of the 'teaching hospital' was never far from my mind, it didn't get in the way of the ongoing journey of faith and obedience that was required for the day-to-day running of the ministry.

Glyndley Manor, the second Ellel centre, had opened in 1990. Our very first long-term programme, the Nine Week School of Evangelism, Healing and Deliverance was also the first activity to be carried out at Glyndley, this exciting new centre, which was to replicate in the south of England the work that God was doing at Ellel Grange in the north.

Jill Southern (or Jill Southern-Jones as she was to become later) was one of those who had attended the second Nine Week School at Glyndley Manor and had been deeply impacted personally by the teaching and ministry. She saw that this was what was needed in the local church and, following the school, decided to organise a healing conference in her local area at Farnham. She asked me to come and teach and bring an Ellel team. A date was set and, without any thought whatsoever that God would supernaturally use this weekend to lead us to the place that would become the 'teaching hospital' for Ellel Ministries, we set out for Farnham.

But this was the weekend when the sale of the buildings of the bankrupt Pierrepont School was announced in the local press. Jill was keen to ask my advice about the potential of the buildings for use by her local church at Frensham and so, before the conference began, Jill, Otto Bixler (the director of our work in Eastern Europe) and I walked up the drive of Pierrepont for the first time on a wet and dark Friday evening.

As the large black and white building came into view it was immediately obvious that this huge place was in no way suitable for the premises of a local church. Unknown to Jill, I turned to Otto and whispered to him, "Otto, this could be the teaching hospital!" Otto didn't disagree.

And so it was that the Pierrepont story began. Jill had no idea at that moment that God was going to call her into Ellel Ministries to pioneer the miraculous acquisition of the property and the development of the work. What followed is recorded in this truly remarkable book. As Jill tells you the story of adventuring with God in an extraordinary journey of faith with Ellel Ministries, you will be challenged, excited and thrilled to see how God took the original vision for a 'teaching hospital' and transformed it into a living, dynamic and vibrant centre under her leadership. Today there are many hundreds of people who have been taught on the NETS programme at Pierrepont, taking the original teaching and training of Ellel Ministries to the far corners of the globe. This book is all about how God used Jill to fulfil the vision.

God chose carefully when He selected Jill for this daunting task. He needed someone whose call was unshakeable and whose determination to press on into God's best, notwithstanding all the difficulties that would be encountered along the way, would not be diminished as the years went by. Jill, with her colourful personality and unquenchable spirit, admirably fitted the job brief. We are so thankful to God for her willingness to journey with the Lord through all the ups and downs of the experience.

While God chose Jill to lead the work at Pierrepont, of course it isn't just Jill's story. I would also like to thank the many hundreds of other people who have contributed to the work, such as the pioneers at Ellel Grange who developed the teaching and training and learned how to bring hope and healing to those in need, sacrificially giving of themselves; everyone who contributed to the prayer and the finances, without which nothing would have been possible; the many staff, workers and young people who have served at Pierrepont over the years – all have played a vital role, large or small, in bringing the vision into being and spreading the Word of God. I thank you all for everything you have done – but above all I give thanks to the Lord for His gracious intervention in giving the vision, and for His constant presence with the team as the work has grown and developed.

I pray that as you read Jill's adventures as leader of the work of Ellel Ministries at Pierrepont, you will be as thrilled by what you read as I am to be writing this foreword to her book. The fruit of that original vision for a 'teaching hospital' has gone round the world – we have so much for which to give thanks and praise to God.

*Peter Horrobin*
Founder and International Director
Ellel Ministries International
January 2015

*Chapter One*

# Let the Vision Begin!

*What is impossible with men is possible with God*

(Luke 18:27)

It was one of those English cold, grey, days. I was working hard on a deadline, so at lunchtime I quickly bought soup and a sandwich and hurried back to my office, close to Big Ben in London. My mind was racing over all that I had to do that afternoon: piles of paperwork, a meeting to attend and employees to speak to. I summoned the lift as usual. When the doors opened, I stepped in, and pressed the button for the fifth floor.

Somewhere between the third and fourth floors, without warning, the lift suddenly stopped and the lights went out. A power cut! Peering through the darkness, nervously I pressed the 'open door' button. There was no response.

Feeling uneasy, I pressed it again.

Still no response.

Aware of a niggling fear, I pressed the same button repeatedly, but to no avail. Trying to focus on the controls and fumbling in the darkness, I managed to locate the red alarm button and pressed it. It worked by electricity, but there was no electricity, so it did nothing!

Panic was mounting every second. I threw my soup and sandwich onto the floor and in a blind frenzy, I started wildly banging any and every button. Go up, Go down, Door open.

Nothing happened.

The silence and stillness closed in on me. Frantically I banged on the doors and shrieked for help: "Let me out, let me out!" The terror and panic in my own voice unnerved me. No one heard and no one came. I was trapped in the darkness.

Way beyond reasoning, I plummeted into a fear that I would never be found in that dark steel lift. There was absolutely no help coming, and no way of screaming in a way someone would hear.

Have you ever bargained with God, your back up against a wall, ready to promise Him anything, as long as He would get you out of there?

I began to pray, "Oh God, if You get me out of here, I promise to serve You completely for the rest of my life. I'll do whatever You want. Just please get me out of this lift!"

In what were just about the longest, most frightening moments of my life, in absolute despair, I crumpled down to the floor. The beating of my heart was so hard, it was almost audible. I started to feel breathless and the thought that I could die from lack of oxygen entered my mind. My panic increased and a cold sweat broke out on my forehead. Tremors deep within moved slowly outwards, affecting my whole being; even my teeth were chattering. I was completely paralysed by fear.

I had experienced panicky feelings before when I was in a confined space, but nothing like this. I was a born-again believer, baptised in the Holy Spirit. God had given me the gift of tongues. I loved the Word of God and I belonged to Jesus. So I tried to cry out to God, but now no sound came. Where was He in this?

An accusing voice in my mind rose to the forefront, "Call yourself a Christian! Trusting God for eternal safety and security, are you? So, how come you can't trust Him in this lift? He is not interested in you, not now, in this moment of your deepest need. Where is your God? You will die in this lift."

It felt very true because as I tried to look up there was no fan, there was no hole. It was door-to-door metal. And I thought, "I'm going to die in this lift!" The enemy tells us lies when we are most vulnerable and least able to handle those lies.

I tried to get myself together and think, "I'm not going to believe this lie." I knew enough about the Scriptures to realise that I was hearing the voice of the accuser of the brethren (See Revelation 12:10). But even though I recognised the tactics of the enemy, it didn't help me. By now I was traumatised and irrational.

I spent four long, terrible hours in the darkness of that lift.

After what seemed like an eternity, I heard a quiet voice: "Is there anyone in the lift?"

My heart leapt. Help at last! I tried to stand up but I couldn't move. My legs felt like jelly and they would not support my body.

I managed to gather enough self-control to try to shout, "I'm in here. Please let me out!" Though they were my words, I didn't recognise my own voice, a pathetic and feeble cry for help.

The next bit was just as bad, because there was still no electricity, so they had to wind the lift up by hand. Of course, inside a lift, there's nothing, absolutely nothing to hang on to. As they struggled to wind it up I was thrown about, and it felt like certain death.

Finally they got it to the next floor and they prised open the doors. A cheery voice said, "Give me your hand and I'll help you out."

Now, when you're a claustrophobic, as soon as you see that escape exit, you want to get out. But there was another problem, I couldn't move. For four hours I had sat on the floor of that lift and become completely traumatised. My teeth were still chattering, I was still shaking all over. I wasn't just shaking on the outside, I was shaking on the inside. I had got completely into shock. So they half-dragged and half-pulled me out of the lift, sat me on a chair and gave me a cup of tea. Of course, I couldn't even get the cup to my mouth because my hand was shaking so much and I felt sick.

My managing director came out and said, "Jill, you really should not be having this over-the-top reaction from simply getting stuck in a lift. Go home and sort it out." Well, that wasn't really very helpful. As a senior member of staff, I felt very ashamed and I took the whole of the next week off work.

Once home, I started to recover. I reached for my Bible and read Psalm 91, "You will not fear" (v. 5).

I was a Bible-believing Christian. So, why did the reality of my life in a moment of crisis not match up to what the Word of God declares?

I thought, "If Jesus said 'It is finished', then somewhere in the finished work of the cross there must be something that I have not applied in my experience. Because I know that I'm saved."

I had been baptised with the Holy Spirit and I was baptised in water. I knew I was a believer. I shared the gospel with others, I was working in the church, I loved the Lord; and yet I could be reduced to a gibbering wreck in certain circumstances. I knew that the Lord Jesus Christ had died on the cross to save me and to defeat Satan and all his works. I knew Jesus had done a *finished* work at Calvary (John 19:30). So, I concluded, there *must be* an answer in Jesus.

Several days later I paid a visit to the pastor of my home church. He was a good man, a lovely conservative evangelical. I poured out my story and he prayed for me: "Dear Lord, please take Jill's fears away."

He encouraged me to avoid all potentially claustrophobic situations. That meant I would now have to use the stairs to get to my office on the fifth floor each working day. Well, at least I would get fit! My pastor told me that the truth sets us free and that I should read my Bible more. I read several chapters of both the Old and New Testament each day.

4

## TRAPPED AGAIN

Several months later, I was with the same managing director and some important clients, in an underground train in the rush hour. It was full of people and all the seats were taken, so we were standing up, holding on to straps from the ceiling. Suddenly the train stopped in a deep tunnel and the engine cut out.

The now-familiar panic began to rise. The crowded train became increasingly hot and stuffy. Other commuters were pressing in against me, stifling me. The trapped feeling intensified to such an extent that I could no longer bear it. I panicked. I had to get out!

We were supposed to be impressing these clients. My mother had brought me up: "Do not make a fuss in public. Just stuff it down, get a grip." My managing director was still talking to these two clients when the fear overwhelmed me and I suddenly shrieked, "Let me off, let me off, I want to get off now!"

I ran to the doors. You feel extremely strong when you are like that. I felt as if I could have lifted those doors off by the hinges. I was trying to get out of this train. Then the lights went out!

A lady came up to me and said, "Look here, love, I get this train a lot and it's probably just a signal failure. Now, just think about it; it would be completely irrational for you to open those doors, because we're on an electric line, we're in a tunnel and we're underneath the River Thames."

I don't know whether she thought she was helping me, but the more detail she told me about my predicament, the worse I felt. Eventually the train lurched forward. I was not looking at my managing director now, you can be sure, and at the next stop I got out.

At that time I had never been back in a lift, because having got stuck in there, wild horses would never have got me back into any sort of lift. Either I walked or I didn't go. So ignoring the lift I ran up the stairs like an Olympic sprinter. You'd never believe I could run so fast! Up the next lot of stairs. Finally I got outside the station, put my head on the tarmac pavement and said, "Oh God, thank You for rescuing me from that train!" My heart was still pounding in my chest with the fear of it. "I'll never get in a lift again and I'll never get on an underground train again in my life."

My immediate problem now was: "Where am I and how can I get home?"

I caught a bus, and the journey home took two and a half miserable hours. Fear is progressive. It's like a big bully, and on that day, fear was gaining more control over my life. Now I had to avoid tube trains as well as lifts.

On Monday morning I had to go back to work and face my managing director. I felt so ashamed, I thought, "I'll get in early." So about 7.20am I arrived at the office. We normally started at 9am. I was walking into my office when his door flew open. "Jill, in my office, now!"

I thought "This is it! I'm going to get the sack."

He said, "I am so ashamed of you. Whatever happened to you on Friday?" He continued, "This claustrophobia thing is becoming major and you have got to get it sorted out. Perhaps you should see a psychiatrist." (I thought: a psychiatrist! I don't think so!) Then he added, "And you're a Christian as well." Of course, that really was the last straw.

So now I was desperate.

I came to God and I said, "Oh Lord, I really, really, really need You to rescue me from this. I don't know where the answer is. I'll go anywhere, I'll see anybody, but I need You to show me. Expose the root of this and get me into freedom."

I began to write out by hand every single Scripture reference to fear. I found 366 Bible verses that tell us not to fear. That is one for every day of the year, including a leap year. I carried those verses in my handbag and whenever a panic attack began, I would speak them out loud.

"Perfect love casts out all fear." (1 John 4:18)

"I have not been given a spirit of fear." (2 Timothy 1:7)

There was only one problem. Speaking out the truth alone did not set me free.

The bondage to paralysing fear remained.

I went to nearly everybody who would pray for anybody, and I went right across the denominations in England. I went to somebody and I asked, "Do you think it's possible I've got a spirit of fear?" They told me, "Either you're a Christian and you can't have a demon or if you've got a demon, then you can't be a Christian."[1]

Well, I knew I was a Christian, so I abandoned the idea that it was a demon and continued going to different people to pray. I was told to love God more, read my Bible more, pray more and to exercise faith instead of unbelief in fearful situations. Nothing helped the claustrophobia. Nobody that I knew of in England had got the answer.

I was being taught that Christians could not have a spirit of fear, and yet I knew this bondage did not come out of God's heart!

So, where did it come from?

## PRAYER PARTNER

Some months later I met as usual with my prayer partner, Sheila Ford-Young, who very excitedly showed me an advertisement for a conference in Brighton called 'The Battle Belongs to the Lord'. It was organised by Ellel Ministries[2] and Bill Subritsky[3] was speaking. Among other subjects being taught at the conference was Freedom from Fear. I booked immediately!

So, in June 1990 I found myself in Brighton, along with my husband, Ron, and my friend from church, Beryl Graham. We listened to Bill, the speaker, saying, "If you are a Christian and you know you are being controlled by fear and you want to walk out from here *fear free*, please stand!"

I had *consistently* cried out to God to hear my prayer and to set me free from fear. Was this my moment to receive God's answer? I leapt to my feet and was amazed to find I was accompanied by what seemed like 1,000 other people, also standing.

Bill spoke about the possibility of things like fear coming down a family line and that it was unlikely that we were the first ones in our family to suffer in this way.

Memories flashed into my mind.

My grandmother was so terrified of being mistakenly put in her coffin whilst still alive that she had requested her wrists be cut after death to ensure this did not happen.

My mother was claustrophobic, and one of my earliest memories, aged three, was of holding a public toilet door open for her to ensure it did not shut.

More recently, whilst in a car park lift, my five-year-old granddaughter had said, "I don't like lifts. Please hold my hand, I'm scared." I had never told my granddaughter about my fear of lifts.

I recognised the truth of what Bill was saying here.

Then he told us that, very often, fear can be rooted in occult activity if people have got into occult things. Often it's not themselves, but one of their ancestors who has done so; it is on their generational line. It wasn't long before he mentioned Freemasonry. My father was a Freemason, so I thought, "Wow, I wonder whether that's the root of my fear."

He called us out to the front, those of us who wanted prayer for fear. I started to be fearful that it wouldn't work for me. First I was afraid that I wasn't going to get free and then, when I was being prayed for, I was fearful that something *would* happen!

A member of the prayer team came along and I told her I had come for prayer about fear. She said, "Jill, OK, I'm just going to listen to God for you." Now, of all the thirty or forty different people who had prayed for me, right across England and from many different denominations, this was the first person who had said

"I'm going to listen to God." I thought, "Gosh, she's got a hotline to the Almighty!"

Then she said, "Jill, I believe God is saying that your fear is rooted in Freemasonry and there's someone in your close family who is a Freemason."

I said, "Well, it's my father."

Bill Subritsky was coming along and praying for people. He asked my lady, "What's this?" and she said, "Freemasonry." So he turned to me and addressed spirits of Freemasonry, commanding them to leave me.

Something happened in me; something you just couldn't control. Out of my mouth came a scream. Now, I'm not a screamer. Remember, my mother had brought me up not to make a fuss, so I'd never screamed in public in my life, but out of my mouth came this ear-piercing scream. Something about it was different. As he addressed the spirits, not only did it come out, but just like the sound when an aircraft comes over and goes off, this scream went out of my mouth and out. I knew something had left.

Bill went off to see somebody else and the lady stayed with me; she was very gentle, thankfully. She sat me on a chair because I was really shaking. I said, "But I didn't stand for Freemasonry. I stood for fear; claustrophobic fear."

She said, "Don't worry. I'm now going to pray for your fear."

As we sat there, she said, "Everything that's linked or attached to claustrophobia, I address you in Jesus' name and tell you to go." This time I just took a very deep breath and breathed out heavily. There was no scream attached to it. Obviously the roots had gone and my spirit of fear just went from me quietly. A deep peace and sense of the love of Jesus for me filled my heart. I knew I was being set free.

The prayer counsellor was so kind and understanding. Whenever there's a spirit, there will be emotional and spiritual damage which gave that spirit rights to get in. So she started to minister into the inner healing that I needed, too. She prayed for the healing of my emotions, including those which had been traumatised during the experiences of being trapped.

By the time she finished, I knew I was free.

People all around the conference centre were also experiencing healing. The presence of God was very powerful. We went on to a wonderful time of praise and worship. I was saying, "Oh Lord, I'm just so thankful, I know I'm different. I know that I'm free from this horrible fear that has completely held me back. Lord, I'm just so thankful to You for setting me free today."

## CALL TO OBEDIENCE

As I was just worshipping the Lord, the woman who had ministered to me came back and said, "Jill, I've been listening to God for you." I thought, "Well, she was right the first time so I'm listening now." She said, "I believe God is saying that you have been set free to declare freedom to others. If God called you into the healing ministry, would you be obedient to go?"

A healing ministry! Me? That was a new concept to me. Yet, as she walked away, the words I had said to God when I was trapped in the lift flashed into my mind: "Oh God, if You get me out of here, I promise to serve You completely for the rest of my life. I'll do whatever You want."

Certainly I wanted to be obedient to whatever God asked of me, but I had a very exciting job in sales and marketing in central London. I had to admit, I did not want to give up that job. And I knew I wouldn't give up that job unless it really was the calling of God.

What I said to her was, "If God calls me, then I will need to know that it's God. It can't be somebody else's good idea. I will need to 'know that I know' that it's God. But if God calls me, yes, I'll be obedient."

## TESTING THE HEALING

Back at work the very next day after the Brighton conference, I was scheduled to do a sales presentation in the John Moores building in Liverpool. On arrival at the reception desk, I learned that I was expected to take the lift up to the top of that very tall building. I think it was twenty floors.

My first reaction was, "I can't do this!" And the lift was the tiniest lift you ever saw! You would have struggled to fit two people into it.

At the Brighton conference I had been warned that I would have to choose to walk in the good of what God had done for me. So I got in the lift, choosing to say, "I will be at peace in this lift whatever happens. I have been healed. I no longer have to fear anything."

It was totally amazing.

Here I was, all alone, going up in the tiny lift, floor after floor.

Reaching my destination floor and getting out of the lift, I realised this was the first time I had experienced no fear when in a lift. This was a surprise, but a pleasant surprise. I knew that something had changed in my heart and mind, and I knew it was something I could not have caused to happen. At last I was free from the controlling fear that had robbed me of a simple freedom! This made me determined to learn more about how God heals His people in this day and age, and I was intrigued to know more about Ellel Ministries.

## ELLEL MINISTRIES

Until Sheila Ford-Young told me about the Brighton conference in 1990, I had never heard of Ellel Ministries. At that conference,

Beryl, Ron and I also heard a man named Peter Horrobin speak. We learned that Peter was the founder and international director of Ellel Ministries.

In 1986, Peter was led to purchase a large manor house called Ellel Grange, which is named after and located in the village of Ellel, near Lancaster, England. The name Ellel Ministries comes from Ellel Grange. The word Ellel means 'All Hail' in old English. In Hebrew it means 'towards God' and in Mandarin Chinese it means 'love flowing outwards'.

Before visiting Ellel Grange, I had heard it was a beautiful mansion, set in large peaceful grounds with one of the finest collections of trees in the north of England. It was bought with a vision that people would come for a 'Healing Retreat'. A Healing Retreat[4] is a time of personal ministry, teaching and prayer. Its purpose is to provide a safe place for people to leave their hurried lives for a few days and to do business with God. They can meet with someone experienced in prayer ministry and bring to God the difficult issues of life. The incidents of life may be in the past, but the pain is still felt today.

As more people learned about Ellel, the demand for this healing ministry grew, and it wasn't long before another centre was needed, this time in the south of England. So, in December 1991, a second centre called Ellel Glyndley Manor was purchased near Eastbourne, Sussex. Glyndley Manor is another beautiful country house, surrounded by parkland and gardens.

At the end of the conference I attended in Brighton, Bill Subritsky had given the Ellel leaders a prophetic word that Ellel Ministries would be powerfully used of God in Russia and Eastern Europe. The fulfilment of this was seen when a small team also started work in Budapest, Hungary, and later purchased Úr Rétje, which was land outside Budapest, for the building of another Ellel centre. Peter's leadership team later discovered that Úr Rétje meant 'the Lord God's Meadow'. Before long, plans were also afoot for a centre near Toronto, Canada.

## TEACHING HOSPITAL

Meanwhile, the numbers of people coming for prayer was increasing and the small teams were working very hard to keep up. Peter knew they needed to train more people to do this kind of prayer ministry. This was not only a need in the UK. There was an increasing demand from all around the world for in-depth, longer term training.

I was to hear many times from Peter Horrobin the words from Luke 10:2 "The harvest is plentiful, but the workers are few."

Peter describes in the Foreword to this book how he was praying about this one night, after many hours of intense ministry, feeling concerned that the ministry team were becoming exhausted and yet there were many thousands of people who needed similar help. As he was drifting off to sleep, God dropped the words "teaching hospital" into his heart. He knew that doctors are trained in teaching hospitals, where they not only attend classes for instruction, but also have hands-on experience of the job. He could see that Ellel Ministries needed something similar, which would provide hands-on training and experience, in addition to in-depth teaching, to equip the Church in the healing ministry of Jesus. And so he started to look out for a suitable place.

There was no doubt that such training was needed, especially for people from other nations, some of whom were making long trips for just one weekend. So Ellel had recently started a nine-week residential training course in healing, evangelism and deliverance. That was a huge increase in length, compared to the previous short courses, and courageously, the team at Glyndley Manor had embraced the vision and pioneered it. It was called the Nine Week School.[5]

## A NEW MINISTRY

On the home front: following my release from nearly paralysing fear, many people in my church and amongst my friends were asking me

13

to pray with them. "How did you get free?" they asked. "Can you pray for me to be set free from my fear?"

The ministry of praying for others grew rapidly. I worked together with Beryl Graham, and we prayed with people. The two of us seemed to be asked to pray with people every spare minute! So many people wanted prayer, both for themselves and for their families.

I attended courses at Glyndley Manor and joined the trainee prayer ministry team there, so I could learn more and grow in this ministry.

At this time, in 1991 to 1992, I was still working in sales and marketing in London. I would finish work on a Friday afternoon and drive from central London to Eastbourne to minister on a Healing Retreat for the whole weekend and then return to work on the Monday.

On one of those early Healing Retreats, a senior lady counsellor called Dr Wyn Owston, gave me a verse from Isaiah 52:11–12:

*Depart, depart, go out from there! Touch no unclean thing! Come out from it and be pure, you who carry the vessels of the LORD. But you will not leave in haste or go in flight; for the LORD will go before you, the God of Israel will be your rear guard.*

Dr Owston asked, "Do you know what it could mean for you?"

I replied, "I suppose it means that I must depart from my job?"[6]

"Yes, I think that's right," she said. "You are carrying the 'vessels of the LORD'. God is gifting you to minister and to teach, and God will hem you in from behind and before."

My husband, Ron, and I decided that we needed confirmation of this before taking any action.

Little did we know it would come on a course entitled 'Moving under the Anointing of the Holy Spirit', held at Glyndley Manor.

## GOD'S CALL

We were actively seeking our next step in God's plan for our lives, and as part of that seeking we attended this course taught by Peter Horrobin. The Holy Spirit impressed upon him to speak from 1 Kings 19 about the call of God on Elisha.

When Elijah put the mantle of the prophet onto Elisha, Elisha responded by burning his ploughing equipment, killing the oxen he was ploughing with, and going to follow Elijah. Peter then said he felt someone on the course needed to respond to this call and completely end the way they were earning their living and go off to follow the God of Elijah.

Ron and I *knew* this was the Lord speaking to us!

Peter asked anyone on the course who thought this word might be for them to stand up.

I stood up, expecting that half the course would be standing with me; but on looking around, I saw I was alone.

Peter anointed me with oil, for *whatever* God had for me. I did not know exactly what this call would entail, and I must say that at this time I had absolutely no idea that it would be to join Ellel Ministries. That was July 1992, and I just knew I wanted to be obedient to whatever it was that God wanted me to do.

Back at work, I spoke with my managing director. I told him about these scriptures and asked to be released when he felt it was right for me to go. After all, the first Scripture verses I received did say that I need not leave in haste or flight.

My managing director read over the verses and sat back in his chair, looking straight at me. "I couldn't follow your God. He's too demanding. But I see this has impacted you, so we'll try to see what we can do."

Finally, in December 1992, I finished my career in sales and marketing. When I left, I still had no clue as to what I would be doing next, except that I had booked into the second Nine Week School at Glyndley Manor, which was due to start in January. When I look back now, it is quite remarkable what happened.

*Chapter Two*

# Dealing with the Ploughing Equipment

*So Elisha ... took his yoke of oxen and slaughtered them. He burned the ploughing equipment to cook the meat and gave it to the people ... Then he set out to follow Elijah and became his attendant*

(1 Kings 19:21)

Somewhere around 29 December I was awakened at about 3am and I sensed God speaking to me: "You have not been completely obedient!"

It was very strong. Shocked, I sat up in bed, then got up, grabbed my towelling robe and my Bible and went downstairs to make a cup of tea.

I sat at the kitchen table and felt drawn to read 1 Kings 19; the passage about the call of Elisha, from which God had spoken to me earlier. I just knew this word was about my own call into full-time service for Him.

As I read again about how Elisha burned all his ploughing equipment and slew his twelve yoke of oxen because he would never be returning to work as a ploughman, I sensed God saying to me: "You have not been completely obedient. What about all those things from your sales career? All those accreditations, the sort of thing you would show to a prospective employer to demonstrate you have a good track record in sales?"

I had many certificates of competence, including sales achievements, sales awards, various commendations and references, my CV and so on.

As I considered this, I knew that all these things should go, but I wasn't quite ready. There were a lot of them and surely it would be quite nice to keep at least some of them?

I read again what Elisha did, and then I did a deal with God. (Don't follow me in this!)

I said, "OK, Lord, here's the deal. If the local rubbish dump is open today, I will get rid of them all, but if it is shut, then I get to keep them."

My expectation was that between Christmas and New Year the recycling centre would be completely closed.

In the morning I put all my certificates, awards, references and so on into twelve large black plastic sacks and set off for the tip.

To my amazement it was open and there were not many people there.

There was a sign by one skip: 'Use This Skip'.

I drove up, opened my car, climbed the metal ladder and threw in the first bag of accreditations.

I continued going to and fro to the car until I came to the final bag. As I stood at the top of the ladder and threw the last bag into the skip, I suddenly fell into the skip myself, propelled by the power of the Holy Spirit.

I lay there for a moment, surrounded by Christmas wrapping paper, wine bottles and turkey bones, and suddenly I had a vision. I saw an angel, twelve feet tall, who was pouring oil into me from a ladle.

The angel spoke and said, "Now the Holy Spirit will be your accreditation!"

And then again: "Now the Holy Spirit will be your accreditation!"

I was really enjoying God's presence and I don't know how long it had gone on for, when a lady also dumping her rubbish came to me and asked, "Are you all right, love? Would you like me to drive you home?"

I got up, still feeling a bit dazed. I had lost my shoe in the rubbish and was trying to get myself together when the lady added, "Never mind. We all drink too much at Christmas!"

I finally got out of there and drove home, feeling so excited about all that lay ahead of me.

At home I read Philippians 3:8–9: "I ... count all things loss for the excellence of the knowledge of Christ Jesus my Lord, for whom I have suffered the loss of all things, and count them as rubbish, that I may gain Christ and be found in Him" (NKJV).

I had to repent that I had considered keeping these foolish things.

How strange that I had done the big thing in leaving my career without knowing what I was going to do, but I had struggled to do the seemingly small thing. As I prayed, I sensed the Lord saying to me that partial obedience is not obedience at all; it is actually disobedience. God always wants the real thing – complete obedience.

## TRAINING TIME

So, at the beginning of 1993, I joined the second Nine Week School at Glyndley Manor. Those nine weeks were a transforming time for me; I received more ministry for myself and was taught and trained on a whole range of subjects related to the healing ministry. Peter did much of the teaching during those nine weeks.

As part of the course, we travelled to the Isle of Wight (an island off the south coast of England) to lead a church weekend. I was quite impacted by this trip, and many dramatic things happened during that special weekend. It was such a privilege to see people in that church community set free from emotional bondages, as well as receiving healing in so many areas of life.

On the ferry coming back, I asked Peter if he would consider coming and leading a conference in my church. Peter agreed, but the first suitable date we could find in his diary was for a year later!

In the meantime, my prayer ministry partner, Beryl Graham, and I continued to minister to people around the clock. Though we were at that age where we still had homes to run and children to consider,[1] people continued to ask us to pray for them. They all came to us via word of mouth, from our church and from our local community. We weren't putting a notice in the paper or even the church bulletin, yet friends of friends were coming for prayer. People began to travel to us, just for this prayer ministry we had learned at Ellel.

We undertook a long-term ministry to a man who had been saved and was coming out of a background in New Age philosophy, which had turned into a complete nightmare for him. We also ministered to a young man who suffered from schizophrenia. We had a major time of ministry to a man who was a paedophile, which included visiting and ministering to him in prison. We saw people join the church because of the counselling and healing ministry. We ministered to literally dozens of people during this year. As I look back, this was a major time of preparation for what was to come, but of course I did not know it at the time.

Beryl and I believed strongly that we needed Peter to come to our area and teach on healing. So many people had asked us where we had learned how to do prayer ministry, and we felt it was time people heard from Peter himself. We felt that the Lord wanted us to hold a weekend where Peter Horrobin would come and teach on God's Word for healing, accompanied by a time of praying for people. We wanted everyone to understand this healing was in the name of the Lord Jesus Christ, and that it had a sound biblical basis.

Finally, in March 1994, after what seemed a very long wait, things were arranged for Peter to come with an Ellel team to our church in the south of England: Frensham Baptist Fellowship in Frensham, near Farnham, Surrey.² Through the local Farnham newspaper, and announcements in many local churches, we invited everyone in the area to attend. We called it 'A Healing Weekend in Farnham!'

There was real anticipation as the date drew near. Beryl and I were the organisers and we recruited and trained a ministry team to help with praying for all who would want prayer during the course of the weekend. To our amazement, 300 people registered for the conference. We quickly realised that our own church building was far too small, so we hired the largest local hall, in a state comprehensive school, Weydon Lane Comprehensive.

## FOR SALE

On the Friday of the conference, I picked up the local newspaper to check our Healing Weekend advertisement, but it was the lead article on the front page that caught my eye. It was about a local public school for boys, which had gone bankrupt and was up for sale. The name of the school was Pierrepont. I had never even been up the drive of Pierrepont School, but I looked intently at the newspaper photo of this attractive mock-Tudor building.

As I looked, I sensed God saying to me, "Take Peter Horrobin to see that school."

I responded, "Well, that is a bit inconvenient, Lord, and this weekend particularly. We have him booked for a healing conference. There won't be a minute to spare."

Our church was looking for a building, as our existing rented facility was too small. This was the reason for my interest in Pierrepont School. I knew that Peter had experience of purchasing old properties, and his advice could certainly be helpful to us. But this really wasn't a convenient moment, so I firmly put the thought out of my mind.

Putting the paper aside, I went over to Beryl's house to go over last-minute details for the weekend. In the midst of the telephone continually ringing with people wanting to attend our conference (we now had a waiting list), Beryl said to me, "Did you see the local paper today?"

"Do you mean our advert?" I asked.

"No, no, no." She shook her head. "Did you see the front page? Pierrepont School is up for sale."

I replied, "Yes!"

She said, "Do you know, when I saw that picture, the Holy Spirit clearly said to me, 'Take Peter Horrobin to see that school.'"

We were learning to be obedient to these promptings from the Holy Spirit, so I sighed, "Well, we had better do it, then!"

I rang Peter to ask if he could come to Farnham earlier, so we could show him the school in the afternoon – while it was still light. But alas, he said that would not be possible. It would be all he could do to get to us in the evening, by which time it would, of course, be getting dark.

## FIRST LOOK AT PIERREPONT

Peter and his team arrived on the Friday evening, the night before the healing weekend. A meeting was planned for that evening in our church hall with all the volunteer prayer ministers, for prayer and a time of teaching from him and to cover all the last-minute notices for the next day. Outside it was absolutely pouring with rain.

Before the meeting, Beryl and I met Peter and Otto Bixler (the director of Ellel Ministries in Hungary), at the end of the Pierrepont School drive, which was just across the road from the church hall. It was quite a battle to get up the drive with our umbrellas. The wind was blowing strongly and the umbrellas were being turned inside out.

"What are we doing here? We must be crazy!" Beryl and I laughed, thinking Peter might find it a challenge to forgive us for bringing him and Otto out in this weather before the prayer meeting. Peter was staying with Mrs Ione Carver, and she had been none too pleased that we were dragging her houseguest out on such a night. She wanted to feed him, and make sure he was rested before he faced the crowds.[3]

Hardly seeing anything in the driving rain, it was dark by the time we arrived at the front door. Even in poor visibility we realised that we were on a very large estate indeed. Clearly this would not be suitable for our little church. We wondered if we had wasted his time.

## THE HEALING CONFERENCE

The healing conference was outstanding. Peter's teaching was excellent, with a powerful anointing of the Holy Spirit; people poured forward for ministry and the prayer team worked hard. People talked for many years afterwards about what God did for them that weekend.

One couple who attended were Dr James Burton, known as 'Mac', and his wife, Peggy. They had been medical missionaries in Africa and on their return had set up a charity called ECHO (Equipment for Charity Hospitals Overseas), which supplied surplus hospital equipment to charitable work in developing nations. As part of this, Mac had become very experienced in fundraising. When Otto Bixler shared at the conference about Ellel's work in Hungary, Mac wondered whether his experience could be of value to Ellel Ministries, and spoke with Otto and Peter about it.

## THE VISION

After the weekend was over, Peter rang us to ask if my husband, Ron, who was a bit of a camera buff, would mind popping over to "that Pierrepont School". He asked Ron to take a few photographs of the school for the Ellel Ministries leadership team. So on a nice day in March 1994, Ron and I went back to the school.

The whole place was locked and shut up. The school, we learned, had gone bankrupt because the bank had foreclosed on them. They desperately needed cash, and so had asked auctioneers to sell off every item in the school individually. The whole place was completely stripped.

There were big 'For Sale' boards up with the name of the estate agent. We had not made an appointment to visit the property, so in a way, we were trespassing. Ron went striding off to many of the buildings on the estate to take photographs. I just stood with my back towards the main house, looking out at the green fields, thinking, "This estate is enormous."

Then suddenly, as I stood looking over the landscape, with the locked doors of the main house behind me, I had a major vision. It was a vision that would prove life-changing for me.

I saw in my spirit a huge globe slowly coming up the drive. The globe was rotating and it stopped, with the country of India right in front of me. This vision was in Technicolor. A door opened on India, and a ladder came out. Many Indians came pouring down the ladder, and I was in a group of people who were welcoming them. We were saying, "Welcome, in the name of Jesus!"

In the vision, we went into the main house (in reality, I had never been inside). We went in with the people from India and as we entered I saw we were walking on a mosaic floor with some pieces missing. I saw a great hall with oak panelling on the walls, a minstrel's gallery, an ornate fireplace and stained-glass windows. There was a real hubbub of excitement. I could sense that the people were very happy to be at Pierrepont.

Still in my vision, I went outside and the globe turned, so I was looking at Africa. Doors opened in all the nations of Africa and ladders came out. Then people came down the ladders. Gradually, as the globe rotated, doors opened on every nation in the world, and ladders came out with people streaming from the globe into Pierrepont. They stayed for quite a long time and then, eventually, they left Pierrepont, and went back up the ladders into their countries of origin. The doors shut and when everyone was safely inside the globe, it slowly rotated back down the drive.

I was left blinking and thinking, "What was *that* all about?"

I sensed God saying to me, "I am going to put Pierrepont into Ellel Ministries. And I am asking *you* to lead the work here."

Oh, my word!

In my own mind, I had no desire at all to take on any leadership of this huge, derelict estate. The school estate was like a small village, and everywhere you looked, it needed money invested and time spent on it. But *in my spirit* I had a sense of real excitement and, of course, a great desire to know the answer to a burning question: Was that vision true? Had I really just seen inside the house? Did it actually look like that inside?

I needed to know. What's more, I needed to know *now*!

I ran to find Ron and told him what had just happened. Finding an envelope in my pocket, I sketched for him what I had seen of the inside of the house. Both of us wanted to know whether the inside of the main house was as I described it. I started to wonder if my vision was really from God, or if I had eaten too much blue cheese the night before!

Ron and I went in search of someone with keys to the main house, and we found the caretaker, Bill Walker. Using some of my sales and marketing skills, I managed to talk him into letting us into the building. As soon as the door swung open, I rushed past Bill into the Great Hall. Tears ran down my face. I gazed at the oak panelling, the ornate fireplace, the minstrel's gallery... it was all *exactly* as I had seen it in the vision, even down to the mosaic floor on the way in, with some little pieces missing.

Ron and I went home, feeling completely overwhelmed.

## TELLING PETER

I rang Peter (who was in Hong Kong that day), and told him about my vision, but I did *not* tell him that God had said I was to establish the work at Pierrepont. First of all, choosing leaders was obviously Peter's role, not mine, and secondly, I was not even sure yet whether I was going to be obedient to God. Peter seemed to feel that what I had seen fitted in with his larger vision of an international training centre. Unknown to me, when we had taken him to see Pierrepont, he had wondered whether this could be the 'teaching hospital' they were looking for. However, he said Ellel did not have any money, so a miracle would be needed. Indeed, the reality was that Ellel Ministries was already financially stretched with work at Ellel Grange, Glyndley Manor, Canada and Eastern Europe.

Whenever things seem to be a little wild, it is a good idea to pray, so I simply said I would be willing to form a prayer group to help bring the vision into fruition.

## THE BURTONS

Around that time, Peter went to see Mac and Peggy Burton, the retired medical missionaries, and told them about Pierrepont.

"The estate is very big," said Peter. "Too big for the church, but I'm thinking it might make a fine international centre for Ellel. We haven't got that sort of money and it really seems impossible to think about it, but somehow I can't get my mind away from it."

"It's not impossible," replied Mac. "All things are possible with God, if it is His plan. If He wants Pierrepont for Ellel's international centre, it won't be impossible."

Peter hesitated for a moment. "If we *do* consider this place, we would be more than thankful to have your help and advice with the fundraising for it. You have such a wealth of experience."

That idea was something of a bombshell to Mac and Peggy, who up until then had been thinking along the lines of helping Ellel Hungary, but as they prayed, they felt an excitement from the Lord. Yes, this really was from God!

So Ron and I, together with Mac and Peggy, formed the nucleus of the newly formed prayer and action committee for Pierrepont.

What happened next proved to be a stunning move of God.

*Chapter Three*

# Three Good Reasons

*We are setting out for the place about which the* LORD *said,*
*"I will give it to you"*

(Numbers 10:29)

Mac Burton and I went up to London to see the estate agents.

"It's sealed bids," explained the agent. "Each person interested needs to put in a bid. At the moment there are fifteen parties who are interested and one has already put in an offer between £1.75 and £2 million."

Ellel could not delay in making a decision.

Peter had gone to the work in Hungary for two weeks, and the only means of contacting him was by fax. If he decided that Ellel Ministries wanted to go ahead with the purchase, we must get his permission to put in an offer in excess of £2 million. If he agreed, we would also need a 10 per cent deposit in the region of £200,000. What should we do? The fax was sent and priority number one was prayer.

A group of twelve of us prayer-walked the thirty-five acre estate; traipsing through the old kitchen which would have been condemned as unusable, climbing up the stairs of the main house which had more than seventy rooms, and just staring at the swimming pool, the sports hall, the courtyard with clock tower, the Oak Tree Court teaching complex and the old computer centre. I stood silent at the River Wey that ran through the spectacular grounds of wild flowers and oak trees. What once was a boys' school, numbering Jonny Wilkinson[1] of English rugby fame as one of its old boys, now stood empty. What did God have in mind?

However, as Peter Horrobin was to remind us many times, if God was in this, He would open or shut the doors, even though there was no money.'

"Lord, if this is You, please help us."

As we waited 'patiently' for a reply to our fax, I had an idea.

I said to Mac, "I think we should send a letter to the vendor's solicitor, explaining what we plan to do with the property and why the family who are selling Pierrepont should sell the property to us."

I had heard that developers were interested in the site for putting up houses and I suspected the sellers would not want the place to be used in this way. He agreed.

I could put my sales and marketing training to use here! I may never have put in a major bid before, but I knew how to set out a proposal for sales. I quickly sat down and thought of three good reasons why the family should sell the school to Ellel Ministries.

## One

Firstly, we were not going to dig up the land and develop it – which was the plan in many of the other bids. Anyone who wanted to develop the land, constructing houses or businesses, could be held up in red tape and official paperwork, and might not have their proposals approved by the town council. We, on the other hand, would keep the estate much as it was. This was an excellent 'why they should sell the estate to us' point in our favour.

This was an aspect of our bid that I believe was important to the family that was selling the estate. This land meant something to them, and from the discussions with the solicitors, it seemed their sale of the land was not all about money. Our bid would keep the land and buildings intact. We would not destroy all they had built over the years and we would actually restore and improve the buildings, rather than tear them down.

### Two

Linked to the hopes and desires of this family for Pierrepont was their care for the long-term caretaker and his wife. In the old and often noble tradition of taking care of those who have cared for you, the owners were impressed that we promised to look after the caretaker, Bill Walker, and his family. We would continue his employment, and house him at Pierrepont.

### Three

Thirdly, we were going to use the premises for good works of helping sick people, not just to make a profit. I just knew this might be important to the owners. They could be pleased that the good name of Pierrepont would live on.

I concluded: "We expect that in the very near future, the director of Ellel Ministries, Mr Peter Horrobin, will be in a position to make an attractive and firm offer to you."

## WE NEED WISDOM

In the meantime, there was a long delay in getting a definite answer from Peter. He needed to discuss the situation with the other leaders of the ministry. The Ellel Executive Leadership group were the ones who would make this decision. Not everyone was as sure as he was about this. We waited and waited, being sustained by many encouraging scriptures.

*The LORD your God himself will cross over ahead of you ... and you will take possession of their land.*

(Deuteronomy 31:3)

*You have stayed long enough ... Break camp and advance into the hill country ... See, I have given you this land.*

(Deuteronomy 1:6–8)

There were many other similar verses.

The next few weeks seemed to be filled with meetings, telephone calls and fax messages.

On 24 May, the first bombshell came. The agents informed us that the deadline for Ellel's decision on Pierrepont was to be 1 June. That meant we only had a few days. Now the phone and fax really did buzz as messages whizzed to and fro in our cliffhanger situation.

We decided to ask the agents to extend the deadline to 15 June, which was agreed. Peter asked us how much we thought Ellel should bid. None of us really knew what to say. How much was a property like that worth?

I sat down with my Bible and cried out to God. "Lord, please give me a figure. I need a number, Your number, an amount for the bid. I haven't a clue how much to say."

Suddenly He drew my attention to a number on the page, which jumped out at me. Could this be God's answer?

When Peter rang I told him. "I have a figure; it's quite a strange figure. 2150."

Peter said, "That must be £2,150,000."

Everyone thought that sounded about right.

The Executive Leadership group met on 9 June. Their decision excited us, but there was a condition to consider.

"We will go ahead," they said, "if the Lord provides the finance."

We started to try to find people who would support or guarantee the finance of a deposit. Nothing was forthcoming.

The agents granted us another extension, and then another and another. The family who were selling the property wanted to wait for Ellel to bid, because they liked what we proposed to do. This in itself was a miracle, because they had already had offers that were far above the asking price. But our constant delaying was causing much frustration and they wanted an answer.

Tony and Gillian Salter joined our small group. Tony had been in the Forces but had taken early retirement and was willing to be the bursar. His financial input and computer experience were a great help. We were also greatly helped by a friend who was a financial consultant.

## THE GO-AHEAD

The Executive Leadership group met again and apparently with considerable difficulty, a decision was finally reached on 23 July. Yes, with their authority, we could continue pushing doors. We could go ahead with the plan to purchase Pierrepont. We were thrilled!

I asked Peter, "Shall I put that bid in?"

With Peter's authorisation, and on his behalf, I typed my very first letter on Ellel Ministries-headed paper with these words: "I am authorised on behalf of Ellel ministries to bid £2,150,000 for the Pierrepont estate." I sealed the bid and took it personally to the solicitors. Then I headed home.

This was it! Because of the vision of the globe, part of me believed that we were going to get it, but the other part of me was still very worried that one of the other bids would be accepted. I kept going from one end of the stress spectrum to the other as I continued learning how to walk by faith at this 'out of my depth' level. To be honest, I was terrified.

"If they accept the bid," I cried to God, "where on earth will we get the £2,150,000? And if they don't accept the bid, what on earth was the vision of the globe about?"

The telephone rang at three o'clock that afternoon. "We are interested in discussing your bid further. Could you now," they enquired, "give us evidence that you have the £2,150,000 that you are bidding? Can we have some audit trail that you actually possess the money?"

I knew that it was important to walk in the light and not to give a false impression, but at the same time, I also knew a lot hung in the balance.

So I said, "As a charity, obviously we don't have £2,000,000 in the bank account, but if you would give us a period of time to raise this figure, this would be the third Ellel centre in the UK – whenever Ellel Ministries have committed to purchase a centre, we have always bought it."


## THE DEAL

They checked with the owners and phoned back a couple of days later. The solicitor said, "This is the deal. You have one month to provide a third of a million pounds, which is a non-refundable deposit. If you don't complete on the sale later, you will lose the deposit. By the end of the month, if the £333,000 is available, we will exchange contracts and give you another six months to find the rest."

I was absolutely euphoric! It was as if I was four feet off the ground. Ron and I danced around the kitchen – well, I led him. Ron was very unsure of what lay ahead, and he had good reason. A huge financial miracle was needed if the vision God had given me, of people representing every country in the world coming to Pierrepont to be equipped and trained to serve the Lord, was to prove to be true.

I heard later that when they learned of our offer, the rival bidders had increased their offer. But the owners still chose Ellel's bid. The Lord Jesus Christ was victorious!

*Chapter Four*

# Foundations

*For God's gifts and his call are irrevocable*

(Romans 11:29)

When I was thirteen years old, Billy Graham came to London and spoke at the Wembley Stadium. It was 1955, and I was taken to see the great evangelist. This event captivated the whole of Great Britain, hitting the front pages of newspapers, and was the talk of every radio station. Universities and colleges sent busloads to see Rev. Graham, or "Billy" as he was affectionately known. On every street corner, people were talking about this 'crusade'.[1]

I had never seen anything like it in my young life. Standing there in the large arena, it was almost overwhelming to see all the people, to feel the excitement and to hear the opening music of the massed choirs led by Cliff Barrows. George Beverly Shea sang with his famous lilting voice, and I was completely spellbound.

Finally, Billy Graham came to the rostrum to speak before the thousands of us in the stands. He was a very handsome young man, with blond wavy hair, big blue eyes and a booming American voice.

I can remember that he preached: "No man comes to the Father except through Jesus" and "Jesus said I am *the* way, the truth and the life." He said, "Jesus is the *only* way to God. Won't you accept Him as your Lord and Saviour?"

Billy appealed to us to come forward towards the arena stage where he was standing, as a sign that we were accepting Jesus into our lives. The choir sang the hymn 'Just as I Am'.

> Just as I am, without one plea
> But that Thy blood was shed for me
> And that Thou bid'st me come to Thee
> O Lamb of God, I come.[2]

Billy said, "Come! Get out of your seat wherever you are in the arena and come and give your life to Jesus Christ as your personal Saviour."

I immediately left my seat and went to the front. Billy prayed over the people who had come forward, and Christian volunteers began ushering us into counselling rooms. I was part of a huge crowd of people, but eventually I found myself in a room with two counsellors, a husband and wife team that God had prepared for me.

This lovely couple sat me down and started to go through a whole pack of literature. As they began to speak to me about how important my repentance was towards God, I came under deep conviction of my sin. I knew I needed a Saviour. I prayed the sinner's prayer with tears rolling down my face. As I invited Jesus into my heart and life, I had a very powerful experience of His presence and I knew everything would change in my life. I finally came to the Lord,

> Just as I am, and waiting not
> To rid my soul of one dark blot;
> To Thee whose blood can cleanse each spot,
> O Lamb of God, I come, I come![2]

## CHURCH MEMBERSHIP

As it turned out, the couple who led me to the Lord lived quite near my home, and since I didn't already attend a church, they invited me to their church that Sunday, which was the very next day.

After all that excitement, I got home quite late that night to find my mother quite anxious. I explained that I had gone forward at the Billy Graham crusade, and given my life to Jesus Christ.

Mum's response was, "Of course you have, dear. You'll grow out of this... we all do things like this when we are thirteen, but it doesn't last long. Get upstairs to bed!"

The next morning I didn't have the opportunity to tell her that I was being collected for church before a Rolls-Royce car drove up outside our house.

"Who is this?" she exclaimed.

"Oh," I said, somewhat hesitatingly, "it's the people collecting me for church this morning."

She raced to the door to welcome the man from the Billy Graham crusade and he introduced himself, saying I had given my life to Christ the night before and he and his wife would like to take me to their church.

"Oh," said my mother, somewhat flabbergasted but managing to put on her poshest English accent. "How lovely. We are so pleased and delighted that Jill has become a Christian."

I couldn't believe my ears. That was definitely not what she had told *me*! And she thanked them for collecting me and asked what time would I be home.

The kind man said "My wife and I would like to take her out to lunch and so it will be early afternoon."

I think my mother would have liked to put her coat on and come too.

As I look back at the foundations of my faith, I am very thankful for that first church, which gave me a great respect for the

Word of God. This couple gave me my first Bible and set me on my first Bible study course with the Navigators.[3] Right from the start of accepting Jesus into my life, I loved God's Word and read it avidly.

## GOD'S CALL IS IRREVOCABLE

After our salvation, I believe the call of God on our lives is the most precious thing we have. God has a calling and a destiny for each one of us, and He never changes His mind over it (Romans 11:29). We can only be disqualified from that destiny if we turn our backs on it. God set this destiny and calling at the beginning of time, and even before I accepted the salvation He had for me, He had begun to reveal His destiny for me in my life.

When I was a little girl of seven, a neighbour asked my mother if she could take me to a slide presentation by a missionary on furlough from Papua New Guinea.[4] I was excited to go and I enjoyed seeing all the pictures of that beautiful country. At the close of the evening the missionary gave an appeal. He asked anyone who sensed God could be calling them to be a missionary to Papua New Guinea to come forward. During the last hymn I immediately went to the front and stood there next to him, though no one else came out. I imagine the missionary was a little disappointed that I was the only person to come forward, a seven-year-old child. He waited at the front, but no one else came, just me. Eventually he came over and sat with me and said, "I'm going to pray that if this is of God, one day, when you're grown up, God will take you to Papua New Guinea to preach His gospel."

I remember returning home and excitedly telling my mother that when I grew up I was going to be a missionary to Papua New Guinea. I actually had no idea what a missionary was, or geographically where Papua New Guinea was located. My mother replied, as mothers often do, "Of course you are, dear," while smiling her 'you'll grow out of it' smile.

## BACK TO EARTH

Years later, as I walked past the old Pierrepont School buildings and thought of the recent vision of the globe, it never crossed my mind that there could be any connection between what God was doing in my life now and the missionary's prayer that day.[5] As I once again walked the thirty-five acres of the former boys' boarding school, my feet were very firmly on the ground in England. I had no thought of travel or teaching in other lands. I simply wondered how on earth we could raise the required funds for the purchase of Pierrepont.

With the substantial costs in mind, a good survey was requested. The surveyors did not find any wood rot or woodworm, or anything like that, which you might expect from old buildings. We were relieved. Of course, they noted a lot of repairs that would be needed to gutters, roof and brickwork. They had good access to inspect the structure, because the whole estate and all the buildings had been completely stripped by the auctioneers. All that was left was the shell of each building. Ellel Grange and Glyndley Manor had been usefully equipped at the time of purchase, but it seemed that God was doing something different at Pierrepont.

## RATTLE THE GATES

Peter Horrobin came down to my house in Surrey, to meet with our small team. He asked Mac to be the full-time fundraiser. I was to be the administrator. Tony was the treasurer. Peter prayed with us that the work would be established from this time on – and, of course, the most urgent thing was to pray for the £333,000.

We began to hold prayer meetings in the Marindin Hall in Frensham, across the street from Pierrepont. We started to pray really earnestly; we were truly rattling on the gates of heaven for £333,000! While we had begun to receive the occasional cheque for £10 or £25, which we were very grateful for, we needed *big* money and fast.

Someone came to me and said, "I have £50,000 in the bank I could lend, but it's my nest egg."

I took a deep breath and said, "You need to know that if you lend us this money and if we are not able to complete on the sale, then you would lose it, because this is a non-refundable deposit. Maybe you need to go back and think about it."

The month went by very fast indeed. There were delays with both solicitors and Ellel's solicitors went on holiday for two weeks. The agents were not amused! There were others who wanted to purchase Pierrepont and they had the cash. They had already offered half a million pounds more than us and were waiting in the wings in case we defaulted on the contract. The agents recommended the vendor to accept their offer.

We continued to pray and to depend on the Lord.

"Oh Lord, help us! We look to you alone."

At this point we received a gift of £5,000 to help with expenses incurred to date. What an encouragement that was.

The deadline was extended because the vendor's solicitors had not yet sent the papers to Ellel's solicitors. That gave us a few more weeks to raise the deposit.

## ANOINTED AND COMMISSIONED

At this point, the three key people in our small committee, Mac, Tony and I, were asked to go up to Ellel Grange to meet the Ellel leadership team to tell them exactly what was happening with Pierrepont. It was important that the leadership was in full agreement with what we were trying to do on their behalf, and were happy with the approach we were taking to secure the funds. It proved to be a long meeting and not everyone thought it was a good idea to proceed with the purchase because of the existing financial commitments within the ministry.

As we waited, they grappled again with the impossibility, the faith risk, the mountain climb that was ahead; everyone needed to be in unity. Not least, there was a real risk to the registered charity that lay behind Ellel Ministries and to the trustees.

Eventually they called us back into a meeting and told us that they had unanimously agreed to continue with the Pierrepont project. They commissioned us and anointed us with oil for establishing the work at Pierrepont. The three of us promised that we would 'hang in there' for the first three years to establish the work, so that there would be a solid core of workers. We shared the vision with the wider Ellel Grange team, and were encouraged by their fervent prayers and their excitement.

## DEADLINE

Many people had caught the vision and there were good numbers of interested people at the prayer support group meetings. Gifts were coming in. Letters were sent out. Scriptures and words encouraged us. We prayer-walked the Pierrepont boundaries. However, time was running out.

On 23 September the agents gave Peter an ultimatum. If the deposit was not paid by three o'clock on Friday, 30 September, the deal was off.

Eventually the night before the deadline arrived. We had received about half of the amount needed for the deposit, but we were still £153,000 short. How were we going to bridge the gap? Only God knew and we were trusting Him completely.

The evening of Thursday 29 September was the regular prayer support group meeting. It was already too late for a cheque, as it would not be processed by the bank in time. We needed the money as 'cleared' funds (available for immediate use), but how could that happen by lunchtime the very next day? We were told it was all too late. Many people crowded into our house. We were on our knees crying out to God, when the telephone rang.

I said to Ron, "Don't answer the phone. We're praying."

The telephone stopped and we carried on praying loudly, crying out!

The telephone rang again and Ron got up to answer it. It was a Christian who lived in the nearby town of Guildford, whom we knew only slightly. The man asked Ron, "How much are you short?"

Ron said, "You'd better speak to Jill."

I got to the phone and again the man asked, "How much do you need?"

"It is a lot," I said.

"Define a lot," he replied.

"£153,000." I held my breath.

"God has spoken to me and told me to lend you whatever you need," he said, "so that you can exchange contracts on Pierrepont."

I asked, "Do you realise it is non-returnable if we don't complete the purchase?"

"Yes."

I continued, "This sounds absolutely exciting" (by now the prayer warriors in my house were praying in absolute silence) "but there is one problem. It has to be cleared funds in the solicitor's account by 3pm tomorrow."

"No problem," the man answered. "I am a solicitor and I will go into my London office tomorrow and send it to the vendor's solicitors on the CHAPS service, which is an electronic money transfer service. So, it will be cleared funds tomorrow."

I went back to the meeting and broke the news. The people who had been praying very passionately for this answer to prayer were now *completely stunned*; some started to cry, and then we all began to sing "To God Be the Glory". When the money made its way to the vendor's solicitor's account, I don't know who was more surprised – them or us.

## AND NOW WE NEED £2 MILLION

Having paid the deposit, Ellel Ministries was now committed and our small team needed to raise nearly £2 million in less than three months. It seemed impossible, but God had miraculously brought us this far, so He would not let us down. He encouraged us and urged us forward through His Word: "out of his glorious, unlimited resources he will give you the mighty inner strengthening of his Holy Spirit" (Ephesians 3:16, Living Bible); "Show his glory to the nations! Tell everyone about his miracles. For the Lord is great and should be highly praised; He is to be held in awe above all gods" (1 Chronicles 16:24–25, Living Bible).

Mac and Peggy Burton felt led to sell their bungalow and move forward in faith to take up residence at Oakhurst, a four-bedroom house on the Pierrepont estate, which meant we would have someone on site to keep an eye on the estate. It was not an easy decision, as, because of a drop in the housing market, the sale involved a considerable loss of finance for them. But with faith and obedience, they followed the Lord and rented Oakhurst from the vendor, and we were then able to locate our offices and literature store there.

Peter produced an excellent appeal brochure to raise the money for Pierrepont as the international training centre for Ellel Ministries. We hoped for some response to that brochure, but almost nothing happened. Time was once again running out.

I started to pray, "Lord, all these people have lent us their money and if we don't complete, they're going to lose it."

Even then, the money simply did not come in, and we faced a very challenging situation. Three months came and went, and on behalf of Ellel Ministries we had to write to the vendors asking for more time. They were not happy.

It seemed an impossible task, and many became discouraged. Ellel Ministries lost friends and trustees as we all went through a period of severe testing. Mac, the fundraiser on our team, began to appreciate what a big difference there was between raising money for hospitals in Africa and raising money for a healing and deliverance ministry in the UK. It was a great concern that people had loaned us money on the back of our promise to raise the money and repay their loan.

The time came for us to consider whether to approach a bank for a mortgage. There were a lot of Christians who felt we should not do this, and so we delayed for a while to see what God would do. In any case, it seemed very unlikely that the banks would lend any money to us, because even if they gave us a mortgage to buy Pierrepont, we still needed to show that we could repay the loan. Pierrepont was an empty shell and there would be much more work and equipping to do before we would have a level of income that would keep up with mortgage payments.

If a bank lent us the money, this would be just as big a miracle in some ways as it would be if people gave us the money. Mortgages were severely scrutinised in those days. They were not given out unless the bank actually thought they were going to get their money back.

When you think that we were asking the bank to lend us a million pounds to buy buildings without any furniture, without any of the basic items we would need in order to open our doors and serve those we were called to serve, and that we did not have any visible means of paying back or servicing the loans – it all sounds crazy.

We approached several banks without success, until we got to Barclays bank. I poured out the story of Ellel Ministries so far and my own story about the vision of the globe. When the letter offering the ministry a loan of £1.15 million arrived, I was extremely excited. However, the offer was subject to meeting certain conditions. We had to produce a five-year plan and we had to show just how we thought we were going to be able to make our payments.

## IN THE LIGHT

I had a really clear word from God, saying that He wanted the *foundation for Pierrepont to go in once and to go in straight, that everything had to be done in the light.* Of course, we would all say "Amen!" to that. However, the reality of obedience concerning the foundation was to prove a challenge. Only one person gets entrusted with putting in the foundations, as foundations are very important. Walking in the light meant to me "no fudging" in the difficult issues. Whoever followed would build on those foundations. We had to provide numerous figures for the bank and do it as accurately as possible.

So we made our best stab at the five-year plan they had asked for. I said that the first year was going to be incredibly difficult because we would only charge people for teaching, and we would not charge for personal prayer ministry. It was already an established principle in Ellel Ministries that we do not charge when we pray with people for healing. It was part of the original vision that God had given to Peter even before Ellel Ministries began. However, it was a challenge for us, because in reality we couldn't teach anyone for at least a year because the site was filthy and there was no furniture and no equipment. In fact, there were no staff members, either, to provide helping hands with all that was needed. There was a huge amount of work to be done before we could launch an international training programme.

The bank granted us a complete repayment holiday for the first year, with the interest on this money added onto the mortgage. It looked now as if completion was finally going to happen. The vendors had been very patient. We should have completed by the end of 1994 and we were now into January 1995. But their amazing patience was running out fast.

One morning the telephone rang; it was the bank manager. Very angrily, he told me that the whole mortgage deal was off because the legal searches revealed that 'first charge'[6] on all properties owned by The Christian Trust, which is the legal entity for Ellel Ministries, had been unwittingly granted by someone at Ellel Grange to NatWest bank. NatWest was the Ellel Grange bank. If the borrower fails to make payments as agreed, the lender with a first charge can repossess the property, so there was no way Barclays was going to lend us £1.15 million with a first charge on Pierrepont to NatWest bank!

I couldn't believe it! It was like playing the children's game, snakes and ladders. I had gone up the ladder and now I was well down the snake. We *had* to get the first charge lifted so that NatWest only had first charge over Ellel Grange and Glyndley Manor, to enable Barclays to have first charge over Pierrepont. This was a major undertaking to say the least. We now had a hostile bank and an even more hostile vendor. It was one of those very low moments.

## ENCOURAGEMENT

God's timing of a word of encouragement couldn't have been more perfect. I received a letter from a pastor in the north of England, someone who had received the fundraising literature with a picture of Pierrepont house on the front. He wrote and told us that when he opened the envelope and saw the black and white striped building, he thought, "I know that place!" Back in 1947, the school had allowed the Boys' Covenanters[7] to hold a camp while the school was not in session.

He continued, "In August 1947, I was standing in a tent on the grass outside Pierrepont. During the last evening meeting, I challenged the boys to give their lives to Jesus. As I was waiting for the boys to come out in response to the altar call, God spoke to me and said, 'On the very ground where you're standing now, I am going to bring this whole estate into My Kingdom. People are going to be saved and healed in this place.'"

He was totally amazed that God had said this, as a healing ministry was virtually unheard of in 1947. He went on, "Here we are in 1995, and God is bringing Pierrepont into His Kingdom and to a healing ministry."

## REALITY OF THE BATTLE

The writer of this letter was quite old by now, but his story helped to confirm to us that God had a purpose for Pierrepont and had been leading the way before us. With renewed determination, I started to race around the country in order to facilitate the paperwork, and speed up the progress of the legal and financial aspects of our endeavour. Everything seemed so slow. In the middle of fighting at this practical level, we were very aware that the enemy was contending for this vision.

There were people who opposed the ministry in the media.

The solicitors acting for us were up in Lancaster and our significant contact was on holiday.

The solicitor in Guildford who had loaned us the £153,000 called to say he needed the money back before completion.

As much as I tried to 'Sellotape the deal together', it all seemed to be falling apart.

It was at this point that I was very thankful to God for an unshakable call, first from 1 Kings 19:19–20 and the story of Elijah and Elisha. Like Elisha, I had left my job; there could be no turning back. I had burnt my 'ploughing equipment' and I had said my goodbyes at work.

I was thankful to God too for the other part of the unshakable call, the vision of the globe. Even in a very dark hour, I still sensed in my spirit that God would give us the victory, and Pierrepont would become ours.

We repaid the £153,000 loan out of monies that had been raised, some from donations, some from loans that had been given to help pay the legal fees and the surveyor's fees that had been required for the mortgage offer. I was taking calls daily from the vendors, who were more than a little anxious for us to complete the purchase. As the first charge was in the process of being lifted, the bank agreed that they would still lend us the money, but now there was another problem. We needed £250,000 in personal bank guarantees to underwrite the first three years of our servicing the mortgage. In other words, we had to find five people who would give a bank guarantee from their bank for the value of £50,000 each, so that if we defaulted on paying the mortgage in the first three years, their money could immediately be used to pay the bank. We had very little time and this was *another* Everest to climb.

I asked God to give me the names of five people whom I could personally telephone and ask if they might be willing to help Pierrepont. This meant that they would go on the basis of their own securities and ask their bank to give Barclays a bank guarantee for £50,000; which, obviously, would be a major risk, as we had no track record. Miraculously, each of the five people we approached agreed. This took time to put in place, so there was *another* protracted process before we could complete, and we still needed substantial sums of money in addition to the bank loan.

In the last few days, suddenly everything seemed to happen at once. Large loans were offered unexpectedly from several sources. Several big gifts from individuals came out of the blue, with more from a trust and two large loans from local churches. This all amounted to £225,000 in just two days!

"Lord, this is wonderful!"

It was the end of February 1995. We had finally got over all the hurdles and on 21 February 1995, Ellel Ministries completed the purchase of Pierrepont School.

# THOSE GATES

We had prayed fervently, earnestly calling out to our Lord every step of the way. Nearly exhausted, but exhilarated by all that God was doing, we rang the solicitors once more, this time for the keys. He told us that "all the keys" were with Bill, the caretaker, and that I could go to his house at three o'clock to collect them. With great thanksgiving I drove through the grand gates of Pierrepont, and at five to three, I was on Bill Walker's doorstep.

I told Bill, who lived in one of the buildings now called Bethany, "This whole estate now belongs to Ellel Ministries and I have now come for the keys." I was very excited.

Bill invited me in, and handed over five huge, old-fashioned biscuit tins containing over 900 keys. None of them were labelled. Bill was dyslexic, so he did not have the habit of writing things down, but he knew exactly which key fitted which door. I was to learn a whole new skill called 'key control'.

Every day at five o'clock, for as long as he could remember, Bill would go and close the great iron gates at the front of the estate.

"Today," I said to him proudly, "I will take you down in my car."

When we arrived at the entrance to Pierrepont, we stopped and got out of the car in sheer disbelief. Bill and I were both stunned. There were no gates. No gates! Those large, wrought iron estate gates were just not there. How could it be? I had come in through those gates just before 3pm, and by 5pm those gates were stolen!

Bill started to shake and said, "This is a bad omen. I don't like this, Miss. I've locked those gates every night since I was nineteen years old and the very first day Ellel Ministries owns this estate, the gates get stolen!"

I told Bill not to worry. We got into the car and went back to the office to ring the police. The police came and went to the pub opposite Pierrepont, which at the time was called The Mariners, only to be told that "nobody had seen anything". Here we were on the A287, a main road, not a side road, and nobody saw anything? These were massive gates, adorned with the Pierrepont family crest, and had been at the entrance for many years. No one saw *anything*?

"I don't think you'll see those gates again," said the policeman. "This is not an opportunistic occurrence. Those gates were measured up for a 'customer' and were probably loosened in their anchorage the day before. It would have taken a large truck and probably four strong men to have taken those gates away."

I rang the insurance company, having taken out a very comprehensive insurance on the estate and its buildings. Because we did not have any money, I had felt the need to be well insured. I asked the insurance company to send me a claim form.

"I am sorry, madam," said the insurance agent, "but there is an exclusion clause on gates. That means you cannot claim."

I thought, "Wonderful! The first day with that euphoric sense of final victory over all the obstacles and then something like this – we lose the gates!"

Still, refusing to let the disappearance of the gates overshadow my joy, I went to bed that night feeling quite thrilled that we had finally completed on purchasing the estate, and that nobody who had loaned us the money for the original deposit had lost anything. God really had done a miracle. I gave thanks as my head hit the pillow, trying not to think about the huge job that lay ahead.

For most of the night, I slept well, but in the early hours I heard the bedside phone ring. It was one of our intercessors. She said in a quiet voice, "I have left it to the very earliest time I could possibly ring you. I've been awake most of the night," she continued, "and I have a burden from the Lord to bring you a scripture verse."

I was still half asleep.

She continued, "It's Isaiah 60:11."

I mumbled, trying to wake up, "Forgive me if I don't remember Isaiah 60:11. Can you read it out to me?"

"Your gates will always stand open, they will never be shut, day or night, so that men may bring you the wealth of the nations."

I sat bolt upright in bed. I was not even a tiny bit asleep anymore.

I asked the intercessor, "Do you know about the gates?"

"What gates?"

"Our Pierrepont gates," I said simply.

"No," she replied.

"Well," I explained, "our gates were stolen last night."

This early-rising intercessor, who had been standing to talk on the phone, slid down the wall in her hallway. For some time, she just sat there on the floor with her telephone still in hand.

*Chapter Five*

# Every Knife, Fork and Spoon

*Your gates will always stand open, they will never be shut, day or night, so that men may bring you the wealth of the nations.*

(Isaiah 60:11)

In the Great Hall of Pierrepont there was just a wooden floor with a heap of leaves in the middle – no furniture, no banners, no carpet; absolutely nothing except the windows and the wooden wall panels. Can you imagine what it was like to walk around an empty thirty-five acre estate with nearly £2 million in loans of various sorts to be repaid and with a vision of people representing every country in the world coming to be equipped and trained for Christian ministry? From a practical point of view, it was difficult to see how it would happen.

We did not have one desk, chair or bed. We had only male toilets in the building as it had been a boys' school. The whole estate had been stripped by auctioneers. Nevertheless, I had a sense of excitement in my heart that this was definitely God; this starting from virtually no provision was His provision. I sensed, even on days that seemed absolutely crazy with work and pouring with rain, that this was His chosen starting point for the Ellel Ministries' 'teaching hospital' at Pierrepont.

Though we were full of need, the beauty of God's provision was obvious. It was all around us if we could but see through the debris and decay. The skylight lounge was a beautiful room on the ground floor of Pierrepont house. The room was light and airy, but the skylight leaked like a colander and the surrounding roof was completely rotten. One day we had eight buckets plus a big black dustbin out to catch the water.

We were certainly crying out to God over all that needed to be done. I remember crying out loud, "Oh God! This is Your place, and I don't believe You want us to have holes in Your roof, and it needs mending. This is *Your* roof! Please give us the money to mend *Your* roof."

Amazingly, within three days of this calling out to God about His roof, we received a large cheque from someone who said that the money was specifically for mending the roof! This enabled us to take out the whole of the skylight and replace it with laminated glass, together with a completely new frame.

While I was not (nor ever intend to be) taking God's provision for granted, I was learning more about how to connect with the heart of God in intercession. This sort of prayer is completely different from the type of prayer at some meetings I have been to, where people are tired at the end of the day and we might half-heartedly pray for something on someone's only half thought-out prayer list. We were really crying out to God for our needs – and I found Him to be utterly trustworthy.

## PROPHECY

The Ellel Grange team were really supportive, both financially and through sending workers. For example, John and Helen Kilford, Ruth Dahl, our ministry manager, Lindsey Stanier and Liz Hunt all came from Ellel Grange to join the Pierrepont team.

In the first few weeks of life at Pierrepont, a coachload of people from Ellel Grange came to see Ellel's new baby and to help us pray over the land. They were a little surprised to see just how big the new baby was, but absolutely blown away with excitement and vision for all God was going to do. After a look around, we went into the sports hall. Like the other buildings, it was also completely stripped of furnishings and usable appliances. We had no ladders, no tools, and the large light bulbs that remained high in the ceiling took a while to come on.

This day, with our visitors in the sports hall, we did manage to rustle up coffee and biscuits for our guests. As we prayed and thanked God for Pierrepont, one of the associate prayer ministers, Bill Stewart, brought a prophetic word.

"This is what I believe the Lord is saying," he said:

> I have stripped this place like I strip a tree of every leaf in autumn, and I myself have stripped this particular tree because I am going to clothe this tree with every knife, fork and spoon, because the leaves on this tree are for the healing of the nations.[1]

As I listened to Bill's prophecy, I sensed the truth of all he said in my spirit, and I thought, "This word is truly amazing!"

As everyone left the sports hall, I wondered just how God was going to fulfil that word. At that moment, there was no kitchen or dining room, as the old ones were so derelict they had been condemned by Environmental Health (Food and Hygiene) officials. The quote we had received for the complete refurbishment was over £40,000, so we had no choice but to just shut the kitchen and walk away. Now, Bill Stewart talked about God providing every knife, fork and spoon!

We tried to be inventive and come up with ways we could cater for volunteers who might come to help us clear up and repair buildings, but everywhere we turned it was more work than we had imagined. We had considered putting a sink and cooker into what is now the kitchen, in the building called Cedars. Cedars was formerly the school pottery room and had a gully with water flowing through it in the middle of the floor. Extensive work needed to be done before we could even have somewhere we could *call* a kitchen, never mind thinking about items such as crockery or cutlery.

Many of our supporters were happy to work in these conditions and to come and help on a rota system, but I did want at least to give them a little sustenance. Finally, we found up at Highfield, the headmaster's former house, that there was a fairly usable kitchen. That was the start of our having team meals. We were able to have a main meal at lunchtime for all the volunteers and core team members[2] on base.

## MORE PROBLEMS

The next problem we faced was that there was no fire certification. *Immediately* after we arrived, so did the fire officer, the health and safety inspector and the Environmental Health (Food and Hygiene) inspectors from the local council! They asked us to keep them informed of what we were doing to pass their standards, and made it clear that we had to get certifications before inviting the public to come to Pierrepont. The task seemed to look bigger and bigger and more difficult to achieve.

Another predicament we encountered was the sewage pumps which the previous owners had not told us were in need of repair. Very quickly, I learned that on an estate such as Pierrepont, the owner is responsible for pumping all the effluent to the main sewerage system in the road and *only then* does the public service take over. We discovered that we had two pumping stations, and everything from Cedars had to travel *up* the slope through underground pipes along the whole distance of the estate to the main road. Bad news – the sewage pumping system did not work! That was a major issue we had to deal with urgently, because very soon we found all the effluent backed up.

The main house was filthy, absolutely filthy, and totally uninhabitable. We had a very beautiful building, but it was not only physically dirty, there were parts of the building that had what we called a "yucky" spiritual atmosphere. It was especially "yucky" and unpleasant down by the boiler in the basement. When we walked there we felt sick and sensed that nasty things may have happened in that place. It might have been that people had looked at pornography, or had had fights or even worse down there in the past. I did not know precisely what it was, but I knew we had to spiritually clean as well as physically clean.[3]

Even with all the problems that came one after the other, nothing compared to being hit by a major disaster – the boiler in the main house did not work. On the information we had been given by the estate agents, they had claimed that the larger boiler we now call Big Bertha was functioning. This was simply not true! Big Bertha was a coke boiler that had been converted to gas. All the valves were seized up and when a heating engineer came to do an assessment, he said very firmly, "That boiler is obsolete. It has not worked for a very long time, *and it will never work again.*"

This was a massive blow. Pierrepont house is a two-star listed building[4] and is very beautiful. In my vision of the globe, people had entered the main house and we needed to get the house operational before we could commence the long-term international training programme at Pierrepont. A warm building was essential.

We were given a quote for £30,000 for installing a new central heating system. I just had to walk away from the boiler problem and pray. We didn't have the money for this, and it would cost considerably more than fixing a skylight.

The reality of the state of the buildings came home to me. There had been years of neglect with no investment into the fabric of the school. We couldn't afford to get discouraged. I needed to find what strength I had to begin crying out to God – again. "My help comes from the Lord," I reminded myself in no uncertain terms. "He is my rod and my staff, and will comfort me." "Perfect love drives out fear," I prayed. "He *will* renew my strength!"

## CLEANSING THE GROUND

Peter and the Ellel teams had already learned what we called 'keys' regarding praying over land and buildings. They had taught us these keys on the Nine Week School. Each key was a vital Scripture lesson about the effect of the actions of previous inhabitants on land and buildings (for example, Leviticus 18:27, 2 Chronicles 36:14, Isaiah 24:5, 2 Corinthians 7:1). We recognised the need here at Pierrepont to pray in these key scriptures and so we began to pray throughout the buildings. We were able to pray with real confidence, knowing our spiritual authority in Jesus Christ, as legal owners of this land.

It was early March, and in the main house it was even colder inside than it was outside. With our thick overcoats, gloves and scarves on, we started to pray: "Lord Jesus Christ, we declare *You* are Lord in this place and we speak now in Jesus' name to any spirit that does not bow the knee to Jesus Christ, and we tell you, you have to leave now! We renounce all authority and rights that may have been given to you in the past by previous occupants in this building. We declare that we are now the legal owners and we speak to all demonic power and tell it to go in the name of Jesus."

God gave us the names of many unclean spirits from which the buildings needed to be cleansed: for example, occult spirits, Freemasonry spirits and spirits of bankruptcy. We moved from room to room, and gradually over a period of six weeks, we went into each of the seventy rooms in the building, going right down into the basement. We spiritually cleansed the place in a very powerful way.

Using anointing oil, we put the cross of Jesus on the doorways and the windows, declaring as we went that we dedicated and laid aside every inch of Pierrepont for the glory of the Lord Jesus Christ and for the gospel. We claimed each room and each part of the buildings, and sent out all the contrary spirits. We told them in the name of Jesus that they had to go and must never return.

Next, we took on a major cleansing of the grounds. We went around the perimeter of the base, taking a map and a site plan with us, which we still have today. We recognised that it was completely impossible to secure the Pierrepont base physically, as we had a shallow river bordering one side where someone could actually walk across from the other side without much difficulty. As we walked around the boundaries, we asked the Lord Jesus to secure the base spiritually. We realised our safety had to be spiritual safety, and we have always felt extremely safe at Pierrepont.

We also walked the length of the river, throwing salt into the water to represent cleansing and healing, just as Elisha did.[5] God gave us pictures and words about what had happened previously on the land. We knew that we needed to bless those who cursed us and also to deal with any power that the enemy might have over Pierrepont through words that had been spoken. We prayed through the spiritual consequences of the previous owners' bankruptcy and financial insufficiency; the school had gone bankrupt, and so had another previous owner. We were the next occupiers after the school and we did not want to go bankrupt. We particularly fasted and prayed and took authority over any spirits of poverty or insufficiency, and we continued until we felt it was dealt with.

## THE WEATHER STATION

One day, one of our supporters asked about the small weather station where the boys from the school had measured rainfall, humidity, temperature, wind force etc. She asked if we were going to use it, and I replied, "I don't think we shall have any time to be looking at a weather station."

She told me her son would be very excited to have the weather station if we didn't want it. It was set in concrete, so I asked one of the team members in our Site and Facilities department[6] to dig it up for the lady's son, to bless him. When the weather station was finally dug up, underneath, much to our horror and surprise, we found a glass jar with a lid on and inside was a paper on which all sorts of curses had been written. This had obviously been placed there when Pierrepont was a school. There was a death curse on the headmaster and bankruptcy curses on the school. Quite a lot of what was written we did not understand as it was not written in English. There were also satanic symbols and drawings inside.

As I looked at this, I asked Bill Walker, the caretaker, "What happened to the headmaster?"

"Oh," he replied, "he died of cancer at the age of forty-two."

I knew we must not dismiss curses, for curses could have demonic powers attached to them. But how amazing! We had asked God to reveal to us any place we still needed to pray, and if this supporter's son had not wanted the weather station, it could still be sitting there now.

I called the team together. We smashed the jar and burnt all the paper with the curses. We sang worship songs. We declared again the Lordship of Jesus Christ over every inch of the land. We forgave the people who had written the curses, and in the name of Jesus we broke all demonic power attached to them. Afterwards, it occurred to me that the enemy had wanted those curses deposited into the ground itself. I sensed God asking us to do the opposite, and to deposit the Word of God into the ground.

I bought some plastic plant labels and permanent black marker pens and gave them to the team, suggesting that each person ask God for verses of Scripture for Pierrepont. On the appointed day of prayer and fasting, intercession and warfare for Pierrepont, we marched around, led by a worship leader, singing worship songs, stopping at various places around the perimeter to push the labels into the ground. So we literally put verses of Scripture into the ground to claim it for the Lord. We all became very alert to claiming the actual ground the Lord had given to us, and cleansing it of anything unclean. We had communion at various buildings, inside and outside. As a result, the spiritual atmosphere at Pierrepont significantly changed. I had a word from Scripture, Psalm 125:3: "The sceptre of the wicked will not remain over the land allotted to the righteous..."

## BLESSINGS

Within a month of the prophetic word from Bill Stewart, we were approached by BBC Manchester, who asked if they could hire the empty main house for three days for the screening of a film entitled *Witness Against Hitler*, starring David Jacobi. This gave us some much-needed income.

While we knew it was important to break the power of curses over the estate, it was also important to acknowledge a heritage of blessings. One of the previous owners was a Christian man named Ralph Winstanley Wood. His son-in-law Crawford Davison was a godly man who was a rice merchant. He helped the people of Frensham through a time of financial hardship by supplying them with rice, and his description of the illness and death of his eldest son, Thomas, shows that he was a kind and considerate Christian. While we had much to do in terms of cleaning, repairing and dealing with any ungodly past, there was also a Christian heritage at Pierrepont that we wanted to celebrate.

Pierrepont is a French name that means stone bridge; hence, we decided our logo should say "A living bridge to a needy world". We were, and are, a living bridge to help people in need connect with God, their true healer.

As we were endeavouring to gain an understanding of Pierrepont's past, we never took our eyes off the mission ahead.

Someone brought a couple of beds so that volunteers could stay overnight to work on the land and in the buildings. Another person brought a sofa for the team room. We got down to the task of tackling our very long 'to-do' list.

People used to say, "If you stand next to Jill for two minutes, you will get a job", because there was so much to be done. It was true. People were scared to sit next to me at lunch, as they would end up with another job on their 'to-do' list. It seemed as if I always had at least twenty-six jobs on my list at any one time. Ellel Pierrepont was founded on hard work, but also a sense of excitement at what the Lord was doing. A pioneering spirit!

Finally, in April 1995, after only two months, to our amazement *300 people* came up the drive to Pierrepont for our very first day conference. Peter Horrobin stood to teach on 'The Healing Heart of God'. All who had been involved in the praying, and the cleaning and the clearing out or sorting out, and the finances, stood in wonder at the miracle of a vision beginning to happen. We even served tea.

*Chapter Six*

# From Ministry of Defence to Ministry of Deliverance

*[Jesus] welcomed them and spoke to them about the kingdom of God, and healed those who needed healing*

(Luke 9:11)

Nineteen years earlier, in 1976, Peter Horrobin had had a powerful vision from God that there would be a place – an actual physical location – where people would be healed in spirit, soul and body. This was the model that Jesus set out when He quoted Isaiah 61 in the synagogue in Nazareth. This was what the Church was meant to be doing. The Lord was longing for His Church to be a place of binding up wounds, healing hearts and restoring lives.[1] Ten years later, Ellel Grange near Lancaster was purchased and Peter, along with others, began to embark on seeing the vision fulfilled. The foundational verse was Luke 9:11: "[Jesus] welcomed them and spoke to them about the kingdom of God, and healed those who needed healing."

Peter said, "I must have read Luke 9:11 on many, many occasions before it jumped out of the pages of my Bible and hit me between the eyeballs! At the time I was praying into the future work that God had called me into, and was asking Him what we should teach on the Healing Retreats that would take place at our centre when it was opened. I was looking for God's strategy for the ministry and not my own good ideas.

"It was as if the Holy Spirit arrested me and made me go back and read that particular verse time and time again – until it had become so much a part of me that I would never forget it. And the more I read it, the more I realised that here, in this almost throwaway comment during the story of the feeding of the 5000, there was the key to my own life's calling.

"To welcome (show love), teach (about the Kingdom of God) and to bring healing to people in need, is the foundation stone of Ellel Ministries. It is only when people feel loved, safe and secure that they will really listen with their hearts to the teaching they receive. And it is only when they have received and understood the teaching that they can really apply it in their lives and receive healing."

What a wonderful calling God had given me, to be part of this!

## NOTHING IS WASTED

I firmly believe that *nothing* God has invested in us will ever be lost. Even the skills God had developed in me over the years in marketing and sales were to prove incredibly useful here at Pierrepont. We shut the door on our old lives when He calls us into the new, but our Father keeps what *He* has planted in us and uses it in His Kingdom.

I can remember saying to God when I left my career, "I shut the door on sales and marketing, and finance for business managers and project management. I shut that door behind me and throw away the key and I now go through the new door called the healing ministry." I remember speaking out that scripture: "Brothers [and sisters], I do not consider myself yet to have taken hold of it. But one thing I do: Forgetting what is behind and straining towards what is ahead, I press on towards the goal to win the prize for which God has called me heavenwards in Christ Jesus" (Philippians 3: 13–14).

I think God has an enormous sense of humour. Every single skill I learned back in my business days, God has used in the development of Pierrepont. I can remember arguing with my managing director that I did not want to go on a two-week course to understand how to manage a project. When you are in sales, going on a course means you're going off-territory and you're not earning any commission. So I didn't want to go on a training course, especially for project management. I was in sales! But my manager insisted. I remember trying the argument of "Why on earth would I want to go on a project management course when I am a salesperson, for goodness' sake?" but to no avail. We argued for over two hours. He won. Now, a few years later and feeling totally out of my depth with an overwhelming project, I was very glad I had done that course.

# TADLEY

Here I was, sitting with the Pierrepont prayer support group, which was an open meeting we held on the last Monday of each month, as most Ellel centres do. We were grateful for many faithful supporters, and our prayer list was long. It was decided then that with our first day conference under our belts, we would have an official opening of Pierrepont. We would hold a thanksgiving service. It was April 1995.

It was at that thanksgiving service that a Mr Jim Bluck came to Pierrepont. Jim had been a member of the Ellel Grange prayer support group, prior to moving south because of his job with the UK government's Ministry of Defence (MOD). He was on the mailing list of Ellel supporters living locally, so it was natural that he should be invited to the thanksgiving service.

Jim had been living at a Ministry of Defence hostel at Tadley, near Basingstoke, when the Tesco supermarket chain made an offer to the MOD to buy the land. The hostel where he lived, Boundary Hall, had recently been refurbished. The MOD had agreed to sell and the base at Tadley was now scheduled for demolition.

Jim phoned us to let us know.

"I started to pray," he said, "that God would do everything necessary so that all the spare furniture, beds and all the fixtures and fittings in Boundary Hall would go to Pierrepont. I also sent a letter to the hostel manager, asking him to allow all the spare furniture to go to a charity and I described what I saw of Pierrepont when I visited for the thanksgiving service; that is, a place totally devoid of plumbing, lights and furniture."

Jim informed us that his governor had kindly agreed we could have some beds.

To quote the governor, he said: "If you come quickly, you can have the beds."

Two or three days went past and we had not yet got round to collecting the beds, because life at Pierrepont was quite manic with our enormous "to-do" lists. Jim rang again to chase me up. Did we want these beds or not?

I asked Beryl Graham to go to Tadley with me to investigate. When we arrived, we found that the whole place had been fenced off and Securicor guards were on duty. We could only get in with a pass. I told them we had an appointment, and they let us in.

Inside, there were three great long buildings around a courtyard. It was a hostel, so they had bedrooms, kitchens and carpets. We went into each bedroom and there was a single bed complete with bedding, curtains to match the bedspread, bookshelves, washbasins, showers and radiators. I remarked, "We would certainly like these beds."

The governor said, "They are free and most of them are brand new. You would need to collect them. How many beds do you want?"

"How many are available to us?" I asked quickly.

"Two hundred and twenty beds," came the reply.

"We will have them all," I said.

"If you are going to take the beds, you might as well have the bedding: the pillows, sheets and blankets with the bedspreads," he offered.

I looked at the curtains.

"They match the bedspreads." I pointed to the curtains, and said without batting an eyelid: "So, I would like to take those, too, and the curtain tracks because we haven't got any of those, either. What about the wooden bookshelves? We need them, too."

"Yes, you can take those, but you need to come on Thursday to collect," he responded.

Ecstatic, Beryl and I rushed back to Pierrepont to tell all ten members of our team. We hired forty-ton lorries with drivers and everyone pitched in to supply labour, as we had to pile everything up and load it onto the lorries. It was a massive job and completely exhausting. Everyone worked flat out.

Beryl and I could not believe the provision of all those beds, but we hadn't stopped with the bedrooms. We had continued to walk around the MOD hostel, realising that all their kitchen equipment was stainless steel, which the Food and Hygiene inspectors had told us was essential for our new kitchen. Could we have those, as well?

"You'll have to ask the chap in Whitehall," the governor had answered, and I got the telephone number of the person to contact the very next day.

The man at Whitehall[2] agreed to donate the kitchen and whatever else we wanted for Pierrepont, as we were a registered charity and the MOD was about to send a demolition team to tear it all out anyway. "Just as long as you have it all out of there in two weeks!" he said.

Now, Ellel was holding a national conference in Brighton at the time, so Peter was able to announce from the platform to over 1,000 people that we needed help: "Our little team of ten people at Pierrepont has got the opportunity of going into the MOD hostel and completely stripping it and bringing back free of charge everything they need for Pierrepont. Would any of you be willing to take a week's leave to help? We can put you up, because we now have beds, and we can feed you, but we can't pay anybody. This is going to be a volunteer exercise."

Thirty people volunteered and we set to work. David Cross, who is now deputy international director of Ellel Ministries, took out the stainless steel kitchen at Tadley and transported it to Pierrepont. We were given the sink, the double sink, the cookers, the stainless steel tables, the preparation places and most of the freezers and fridges.

We went on to strip the bedrooms of their electric light fittings and switches, the plugs out of the wall, the mirrors and radiators. We were given copper pipe. We were given 150 toilets and related plumbing items including baths, basins, shower cubicles and fittings, towel rails, shaver fittings and strip lights. We were given dining room equipment and all the round tables and chairs.

The two weeks we were first given by Whitehall turned into six weeks. By this time we were taking out the window frames, the internal doors, everything from the car park, including the lights and light fittings, as well as items in their workshops. We completely stripped the place.

We got to the corridor of Tadley and remembered we had no carpet back at Pierrepont. We desperately wanted the blue and green fleck carpet that we saw all the way down the hallway. Unfortunately, instead of just sticking that carpet at the corners, the carpet fitters had taken black glue and painted it all over the floor and rolled the carpet down on top of the glue. When we tried to pull the carpet up, we couldn't get it away from the floor without losing the rubber backing, rendering it useless.

The men said, "It can't be done."

Everything we and our team of volunteers had taken apart and off the walls day after day had to be lugged down to the lorries and transported over to Pierrepont, and then stored until we could refit. Everyone's back ached from all the hard work, yet we women were determined that we were not going to leave without the carpets. We decided that if we got the women in a row, say six of us, we could start to roll the carpet, taking the backing with it, if we had wallpaper scrapers.

I went with Helen Kilford to buy some scrapers. As we came back into Tadley from our successful shopping expedition, once again we went through the usual MOD security check by the Securicor men. I had a paper bag stuffed with scrapers. One of the guards walked up to me, and picked up my paper bag, probably thinking I had bought doughnuts and he was going to have one for himself. We opened this paper bag for him to check it. As he looked inside, he gasped with horror, "You're not going to take the wallpaper off the walls, are you?"

We all laughed, and someone told the guard not to give us any ideas.

We went and got the carpet, and received with great thankfulness all that was given to us.

If you have ever moved house with a lot of stuff and you are going up and down stairs, you will know that by the end of the day you are on your knees. Even with all our volunteers, we were absolutely exhausted.

Heading back to Pierrepont, I can remember standing at the door of Cedars, waiting for a lorry to arrive with all the stuff loaded on. I had also cooked for the workers and I ached with exhaustion as much as everyone else who had pulled curtains off railings, piled bedding and fixtures onto the back of a lorry or had scraped carpet up on their knees. As I leaned against the door, ready to help with the unloading, suddenly there came a reminder of the words spoken over Pierrepont from Isaiah 60:11: "Your gates will always stand open, they will never be shut, day or night, so that men may bring you the wealth of the nations." With clarity, it hit me that all these things we were receiving were not something that belonged to an ordinary person; this stuff was from the government's Ministry of Defence. This was *the wealth of the nation.* It was moving out of the Ministry of Defence and into the Ministry of Deliverance. It was the wealth *of a nation* coming up the drive and coming in here. Immediately, Bill Stewart's prophecy came pounding into my weary thoughts: "I [the Lord] am going to clothe this tree with every knife, fork and spoon."

I needed to sit down for a moment and take it all in.

*Chapter Seven*

# No Turning Back

*Have I not commanded you? Be strong and of good courage; do not be afraid, nor be dismayed, for the LORD your God is with you wherever you go*

(Joshua 1:9, NKJV)

God loves a good dinner party, I am sure of it. When you think of all that He does over a shared meal... it can be a time of giving credit where credit is due, a time of blessing, a time of unity with sisters and brothers in Christ and a time of witnessing to others. A good dinner party nourishes spirit, soul and body, and a meal in His name can lead to a divine appointment!

One of our supporters had a dinner party on a Saturday. With friends gathered and relaxed around a table, the conversation soon turned to Pierrepont.

"Have you heard what happened at Pierrepont? God is doing something quite extraordinary down there."

They told the story of Tadley, describing how the Lord gave us not just the beds, but the kitchen sink and every item imaginable from a Ministry of Defence hostel. They smiled at the idea of the Ministry of Defence going to the Ministry of Deliverance. What a miracle to equip the whole place so quickly! There was a joy in telling the details, as everyone marvelled over how God had given Ellel Pierrepont so much blessing.

"Of course," said the host, "quite a bit more is needed. They certainly needed everything they got, but they started with nothing. Did you see how Pierrepont was stripped bare when Jill first received the keys?"

"How much did the MOD charge Ellel?"

"Nothing. Pierrepont is a registered charity, so they got it all for free."

"That could only be God."

The guests lingered around the dinner table that night.

## SHELL-BLUE TILES

One of the men gathered around that table worked for the Shell Oil company. On Monday morning as he reported for work, he couldn't get out of his head the story he had heard on Saturday night.

He walked up the Strand in London for an office meeting, and headed to the fifth floor. At that meeting his manager announced that the decision had been made to rent out a whole floor of their office block to another company. Shell workmen had already taken out all the office furniture, but what was left was the Shell-blue carpet tiles. The new people moving in did not want them because blue was not their corporate colour.

The manager asked him to organise for all the carpet tiles to be taken up by a contractor that very next weekend and to have the tiles thrown away.

"I happen to know a charity in Frensham, Surrey, who may be willing to come and take these carpet tiles and use them. Would we be willing to let them do it for nothing, rather than let a contractor take them and charge us for the privilege?" the man asked his manager.

"Yes, that's OK, but don't let the charity take only the good tiles in the middle of the floor. They would need to take the fill-in ones on the edges as well. And they will have to complete the job this weekend."

He phoned me to tell me the proposition. "What do you think, Jill?"

"How many carpet tiles are there?" I asked.

"Fifty tonnes."

I sat at my desk to take stock. I needed to work out how to take fifty tonnes of carpet off a floor in central London and bring them back to Pierrepont. We couldn't just throw them through the door. We needed a plan to know exactly what we were going to do and how we were going to do it, and we only had one weekend to get the tiles. Once again I thanked God for *forcing* me to attend the project management course that I had so vehemently resisted back when I was in sales and marketing. Again I was reminded that nothing that God has invested in us will ever be lost. This was one project that needed to come together quickly. Talk about project management!

I worked out a plan: all the women who would be helping us would be assigned to pick up the individual carpet tiles and put the fuzzy side to fuzzy side in packs of five pairs; so there would be ten carpet tiles in a pack. The men would come and manually pick up the packs of carpet tiles, which could be quite heavy, and carry them into the corridor, where we would use Shell's pump truck (a pallet jack). We would place the carpet tiles on this and pull it to the lift. The lift would take the tiles down to the ground floor and we could pull the pump truck to the loading bay. In the loading bay we would load the tiles into wooden pallets, which we would need to buy.

We would also need to buy industrial cling wrap, and cling wrap the tiles onto the pallets. We would use Shell's forklift truck to lift the pallets, which would now be far too heavy for anyone to lift onto the truck we would need to rent. When we returned to Pierrepont with the carpet tiles, we would need to hire a forklift truck at our end to move the tiles from the truck to the storage site, which was in the building we call Bethany.[1]

With the project all planned, off we went, on the Farnham to Waterloo train with cheap day return tickets. Carrying our packed lunches and excited about the adventure ahead, we walked over Waterloo Bridge to the Shell building on the Strand. When we entered the building and got to the fifth floor, all we could see was acres of floor covered with the blue carpet tiles, which were in extremely good condition. Blue everywhere!

The tiles would have cost £5 each to purchase new, and so with enthusiasm we started picking them up, one at a time. We worked all Friday evening, all day Saturday and all day Sunday. Finally, with sore knees, knuckles and hands, we finished our labour on Sunday night. We had given our all and were mostly asleep on the train coming back, exhausted.

On reflection, I realised I hadn't thought of one small detail in the project plan – work gloves. Still, we were delighted to have the carpet tiles, especially as they are so versatile. You can simply put them down on a wooden floor without underlay, and if the carpet becomes stained or damaged, they can be easily replaced. What a gift![2]

As we returned to Pierrepont, still ahead of us was the task of unpacking the trucks and storing the pallets, but it was done very efficiently. On our small team, there just *happened* to be a young man who *happened* to have a forklift licence. God's hand was on everything.

Nearly the whole of Pierrepont is carpeted with those Shell-blue tiles, including the Cedars dining room and corridors, the coffee lounge in the main house and all the accommodations and offices. These carpet tiles became like the widow's oil (2 Kings 4:1–7), as we gave a large number of the tiles to Blairmore in Scotland,[3] to Ellel Grange for their bookshop, and to Glyndley Manor. All the UK Ellel centres have at least some of the Shell-blue carpet on their floors today. I have often paused to wonder how much it would have cost us to carpet those huge areas if we had not received this miraculous gift. More than twenty years later, we still have some unused Shell-blue carpet tiles in storage at Pierrepont. What an incredible God we serve.

## LAUNDRY

We did have another problem, though; the laundry was piling up! With volunteers staying and working at Pierrepont, the bedding was being used and the sheets needed washing as well as the work clothes. What to do? We had no washing machines, or any way to take on this level of laundry.

I suddenly remembered that while walking around Tadley, I had spotted a number of brand-new Maytag washing machines. Some of them still in their polythene wrappers, never used. I called the man at Whitehall and asked him if we could have them. He said that they were for sale to the highest bidder, but we could submit a bid. Our Pierrepont finance department told me that we could only bid as high as £1,500.

"You'll never get them for that!" said members of the team. "Those are industrial washers, worth about £3,000 each." And there were twelve of these machines, plus eight industrial dryers. Still, I put the bid in for £1,500 and prayed. The whole team prayed for those machines, as we imagined fresh laundry.

Several days went by, and we had no response from Whitehall. Each morning in team prayers, someone would ask, "Had any response to the bid?" and "We'll never get them for that amount!"

On the fourth day we received a fax (no emails in those days) saying we needed to come to collect the twelve industrial washing machines and eight industrial dryers – and could we please send our cheque for £1,500?

God *is so* good!

# TOAD HALL

Out of the blue we had a phone call from a film agency for Shepperton Studios.

They said, "We're looking to make a film, and we wondered whether we could use Pierrepont?"

I said, "I don't think so."

"Why not?" asked the agent.

I replied, "Well, we are a Christian organisation and we probably wouldn't agree with the content of your film."

"What wouldn't you agree with?"

I said, "Well, let me give you a list. If you want to make a film at Pierrepont, it can't have any blasphemy in it; it can't have any sexually explicit scenes in it; it can't have anything occult in it; it can't have anything gratuitously violent in it; I wouldn't want any swearing in it, and that is probably going to take most films out."

The quiet voice at the end of the phone said, "Would *The Wind in the Willows* be alright?"[4]

I had enjoyed reading *The Wind in the Willows* as a child, and so agreed to the filming of this simple, fictional story about a toad, a rat and a mole. This turned out to be more than just a chance to delight in a childhood story; it also brought a surprise blessing: Shepperton Studios promised to send *a cleaning crew* to clean the main house.

When they said they would send cleaners in, I must admit I imagined six or so women with vacuum cleaners, but they sent in a huge army of industrial cleaners with large equipment that cleaned anything and everything. They vacuum-swept the chimneys, both in the Great Hall and the coffee lounge – chimneys which hadn't been swept since who knows when.

They then set about with their chemicals and their power vacuum cleaners and driers, completely cleaning everything in the Great Hall, the stairs and the hallway. They cleaned the ceilings which were black with cobwebs, and thick dust that was way beyond a simple spray and polish. They thoroughly cleaned the coffee lounge, which was to be Toad's bedroom in the film. Everything was clean, just right for a home for Toad. The Great Hall was to be the central attraction.

They cleaned off all the writing the schoolboys had done, such as "PJ loves BH true", and got rid of the deeply scored markings made with geometry sets on the wood panelling. In Toad's bedroom where they filmed more close-up work, they actually waxed all the wood panelling as well. They completely decorated the hall and put some red felt carpeting on the stairs, sprayed it with gold and hung very large portraits of "previous Toads".

At the same time, the studio sent in their own catering team and we benefited from many delicious leftovers. And as if that wasn't enough of a blessing, when they were actually filming, they paid us £2,000 a day! This was so much more than the filming of a children's story. We could feel God's delight in bringing Pierrepont house to life. How incredible of God to clean the whole place for us for nothing!

## BIG BERTHA

But I still had a problem with the heating. An essential part of making this an inviting building, especially in the winter months, was the central heating. We needed to be warm. Coming against all that the heating engineer had told us, we tried to put the boiler on, but it just seized up. For a brief moment, there was a small glimmer of hope that the engineer could be wrong. Was it really obsolete? Would it really never work again? Couldn't it possibly be just another clean-up project? Water and leaves had come in, and there were mice in the old heating system.

Have you ever had someone central to your vision lie to you? We had been told by the previous owners that the heating system was working. But this boiler hadn't suddenly seized up; it had been like this for a long time. The repair men had pronounced our boiler completely obsolete and defunct.

We moved into Pierrepont in March 1994, when it was really cold, with wind and rain. To me, heating was not an optional extra. This had to be sorted. It seemed to be even colder inside the main house than outside, and outside was bitterly cold. As the main house had been empty for so long without heating, it had become the kind of cold that gets into your very bones.

A man named Ian Coates,[5] who was part of the core Ellel Grange team, came down to help us, and joined our Sites and Facilities team. One of the first things I asked Ian to do was to look at the boiler. I took him to see what we were starting to call Big Bertha, the enormous boiler in the basement.

"When it starts to fire up," I told him, "apparently it is supposed to sound like a 747 plane taking off. There are seventy rooms in the main house, and they all need to be heated by this boiler. We've been told that all the valves are completely seized up."

From the first days we had prayed over the boiler room, feeling that there was a spiritual darkness deep in this part of the main house. It wasn't just that the previous owners had misinformed us about Bertha being in working order; our prayer team also had a strong sense that this was an area where we needed to break curses of darkness. What had happened here? We didn't know, but we did know that we needed to fast and pray and break the power of the enemy gained here through whatever had happened in years past that was not godly. So much prayer had gone into the spiritual cleansing of this room, but now we needed someone with the skill to bring the boiler to working life. We needed it to fire up!

Ian Coates looked at the boiler. "Do you know, Jill," he said, as he continued to look at it, "many, many years ago when I was an apprentice, aged fifteen, the very first thing that I ever worked on was this exact model of boiler."

How many people did I know who had actually done an apprenticeship on the very model of the boiler that God had given us?

The only thing I truly knew at that moment was that I had been told the boiler was completely obsolete and no one made it anymore.

Ian said, "Let me have a look at it, and see if we can get it working."

About three days later he came to me and said, "I just have a feeling in the back of my head that perhaps we could un-seize these valves, and instead of having to have a brand-new heating system and a brand-new boiler, which would cost a fortune, we could actually get this one going."

Ian started to pray, and put some WD-40 (a type of spray oil) into the valves. He went away and prayed; he came back and put some more WD-40 in the valves. He went back and forth for days. Prayer and WD-40, prayer and WD-40, prayer and WD-40. Slowly he began to move the valves until gradually over a period of two weeks of praying and applying WD-40 he finally managed to unseize them.

Then we found that the pump was also not working, so Ian had to strip it down and find the one component that wasn't working. That one component was purchased for something like £100, and that got the pump working.

Big Bertha was fired up!

## 100 YEARS OF DUST

The next big problem was that the heat was supposed to come up through brass grilles in the floor. However, the building was over 100 years old and 100 years' worth of dirt and dust had gone through the grilles and had compressed down into something as hard as a brick. No heat could come through or circulate, and so Ian began praying and figuring out once again what to do.

This time, a young Ukrainian on the Young People's Team came to the rescue. He had done some potholing in the past and he offered to have a rope tied onto him and to go with a vacuum cleaner underneath the floor. This was a very tight space and necessitated going the full length of the Great Hall. Thankfully, he was quite thin.

He went on his tummy and he wiggled his way all along, taking out all the dirt and dust under the floor. He crawled beneath the entire ground floor several times, which took him three weeks, vacuuming and getting rid of blockages.

Ian fired up Big Bertha again.

The young Ukrainian came running and found me where I was working at Cedars. "Ian says, 'Come quickly up to the main house, the heating is working!'"

I ran up the drive to the house and, as I came through the front door, a rush of heat hit me. It was just as if the heart of the building itself had started to pump again. With this welcome heat, the heart was saying, "This building is now functioning."

We just stood in the warmth of His love and provision, giving thanks to God once more. It was just so good to be warm!

## NO TURNING BACK

God was giving us lots of material things, everything we needed. Gradually, all the bits and pieces we needed for starting up a centre were coming together. It was like a jigsaw puzzle, but even as we saw piece after piece fitting into place, there was still one major piece missing: actual cash was in short supply.

We had a bank loan, and I had to go back to the bank and explain, "You know we said we needed a year of not making payments? Well, actually, we would like to make that two years. Would that be alright?"

They weren't too pleased but finally agreed to an interest-only arrangement, so we could get ourselves on the road.

Yet, this road was beginning to feel a little lonely. Three people had been commissioned, anointed with oil by the Ellel Ministries leadership and had covenanted with the International Ministry to serve for the first three years of starting Pierrepont. But I was the only one left.

One of them had left earlier and now the other one had just said to me, "We are moving from Farnham."

What could I say? What was there to say? The loneliness of the long-distance run of this vision was quite tough. Yet, as I looked around, I knew people were praying for me. I knew God had answered more than I had even asked. But there was a sadness that was a challenge to shake off. There was a moment of feeling quite alone. As one who had promised to be part of a group anointed for this work of Pierrepont, I was now standing on my own.

At the first birthday of Pierrepont, the team members, volunteers and a number of our supporters gathered for a time of thanksgiving. As I walked into Cedars for this occasion, a young woman was leading worship. Strumming her guitar, she led us in singing:

> I have decided to follow Jesus;
> No turning back, no turning back.
>
> Though none go with me, I still will follow ...
> No turning back, no turning back.[6]

I looked at the birthday cake on the table. As if to symbolise not just Pierrepont's first anniversary, but the thoughts of my heart, it had only one candle. "I know I am called to do this, but it is really tough," I silently prayed.

Still the young woman sang:

The world behind me, the cross before me;
No turning back ...

Sometimes it is very easy to sing worship songs and much more difficult to live out what we sing. I just stopped and said, "Lord, I can't sing this."

I felt God say, "Come on, sing this to Me. Don't fix your eyes on people. This has got to be about you being a woman of faith trusting Me, even when it looks pretty grim."

So, I started singing and giving a fresh declaration over the one little candle: "Though none go with me, I still will follow ... No turning back, no turning back."

*Chapter Eight*

# The Heart of God to the Heart of Man

*but the crowds learned about it and followed him. He welcomed
them and spoke to them about the kingdom of God ...*

(Luke 9:11)

On 1 February 1997, forty-four men and women came up the drive
for our very first international course, which we called NETS. This
was to be a six-month programme, the first time Ellel had offered
such a long training course. It was breathtakingly exciting for us to
meet the new trainees, to badge them up and to try to learn all their
names.

As the first ones were arriving, we were still decorating some of
the rooms. It was completely manic at Pierrepont; decorating, deep
cleaning and all kinds of preparations going on. Who could cook for
this number? Who was going to teach for six months?

Peter Horrobin's vision of an international 'teaching hospital'
where Christians would come to learn how to pray the Word of God
for healing and receive from God for themselves, was about to begin!
My vision of the globe,[1] with people from all over the world coming
to Pierrepont, was actually becoming reality.

The very first trainee up the drive was Diane Watson, who
later became the first director of Ellel Gilbulla in Sydney, Australia

and moved on from there to run the centre in Perth. The trainees arrived from the UK, Poland, New Zealand, USA, Portugal, Switzerland, Australia, Canada, Singapore, Hong Kong, Spain and the Netherlands.

From the beginning, NETS stood for (Luke) Nine Eleven Training School.[2] This verse, Luke 9:11, is the foundational model for the whole of Ellel Ministries. Jesus Himself set the example we are to follow in welcoming people, teaching them about the Kingdom of God and then bringing healing to those who need God's healing. Andy Taylor, who was Peter's PA at the time,[3] suggested NETS and we loved it. Later, on another NETS, someone commented that NETS also stands for Never Ever The Same. How true that is!

At last, here was a 'teaching hospital' that would train 'doctors' for the local church. Here at NETS, through the gracious work of God, they would receive their own healing in spirit, soul and body. Not only that, but each one would be trained in prayer ministry, healing and deliverance. They would take what we were calling 'keys of the Kingdom of God' back to their country of origin to assist in the work of their local church.

The verse we would come to have deep in our hearts was 2 Timothy 2:2: "And the things you have heard me say in the presence of many witnesses entrust to reliable people who will also be qualified to teach others".

We wanted a 'hear, see, do' model. Teachers would share the Word of God with the trainees (hear); then prayer ministry was to be visually demonstrated (see). Finally, the trainees were to practise (do) what they had heard and observed, getting practical experience in healing and deliverance. Always the goal would be Ephesians 4:12: "to prepare God's people for works of service, so that the body of Christ may be built up".

A vital part of NETS was prayer. While we had already prayed through the buildings and the grounds, now with classes about to start we needed to pray over the trainees, their journeys to and

Ellel Grange, where the work of Ellel Ministries began in 1986.

The Battle Belongs to the Lord conference banner.

Bill Subritzky teaching at the Battle Belongs to the Lord.

Peter Horrobin teaching at the Battle Belongs to the Lord.

Joe and Ruth Hawkey. Joe prayed with Jill when she finished the 9-Week School.

*An Ellel Ministries Training Programme*

"Jesus called the twelve disciples together and gave them power and authority to drive out all demons and to cure diseases. Then he sent them out to preach the Kingdom of God and to heal the sick." Luke 9:1-2

# The International School of Evangelism Healing and Deliverance

held at Glyndley Manor, Sussex, England and now Ellel Canada, Orangeville, Ontario.

Two Schools are held each year in the Spring and the Autumn for a nine week period.

In 1995, the Spring School will take place at Ellel Canada.

Glyndley Manor, Stone Cross, Pevensey, Nr. Eastbourne, East Sussex, BN24 5BS, UK

The 9-Week School brochure.

Ellel Glyndley Manor, where Jill atttended the 9-Week School.

Aerial view of Pierrepont.

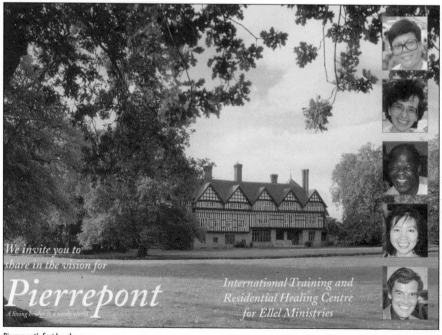

Pierrepont's first brochure.

Bill Walker, Pierrepont groundsman.

Ian Coates by Big Bertha (Main House Boiler).

Jill and Ron Southern at Pierrepont.

The Great Hall as Jill saw it the first time.

Shell carpet tiles being loaded onto the lorry.

Tadley toilets.

The Long Room with the perfectly fitting and colour matching curtains.

God's miraculous provision ...

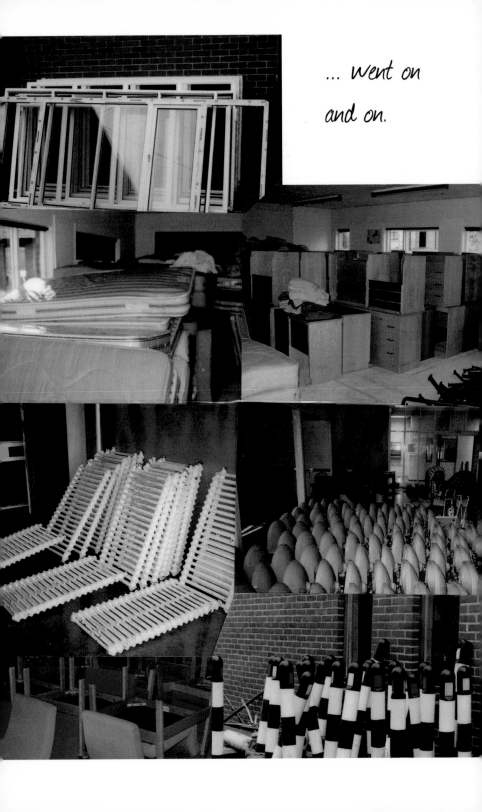

... went on
and on.

The scene at Tadley ...

after the Ellel team ...

... had visited!

Some of the ...

... workforce

... at Tadley

Early days – open day car park.

*The first Pierrepont Conference April 1995*

Group Photo NETS 1, 1996.

Jill with the prayer team who walked the grounds in 1995.

Fred and Barbara Elgar.

Stella & Ione – the dynamic duo.

Bill and Olive Stewart with Peter Horrobin.

Paul & Diane Watson.

John and Helen Kilford.

Ron and Jill with Jim Graham.

John Kilford, Jill, Martin & Ginny Knapp in Sweden in 2001.

NETS 4+ Brochure.

10th Anniversary, from left to right Ron, Jill, Peter and Fiona cutting the cake.

Pierrepont 10th Anniversary celebration.

Inus and Julia Joubert.

The World Map in Cedars.

Pierrepont main house in winter.

NETS teaching in the Great Hall.

George Verwer teaching NETS.

NETS Trainees.

NETS Stage 3 on mission trip in Thailand.

NETS being taught in the Conference Hall.

Jill teaching the very first stage 3 in the Skylight Lounge.

NETS 12 graduation.

The front facade of the Main House at Pierrepont.

Group photo NETS 33.

Jill on teaching tour in Christ Church New Zealand.

Jill teaching NETS in the Great Hall.

Colin and Jill.

'Jesus Heals' free day – worship.

Tea Break in the sunshine during a Free Teaching Day.

Pierrepont rear facade.

Ellel International Leaders Conference 2014 – all those who have done NETS.

Oak Tree Court. Former classrooms, now housing bedroom accommodation.

The entrance to Pierrepont House – from where the gates were stolen.

"But for you who revere My name, the sun of righteousness will rise with healing in its wings" (Malachi 4:2). Pierrepont Great Hall 1994.

from our centre, and about the curriculum; as well as pray about *how* we should share the life-changing keys of the Kingdom of God with those who came to Pierrepont.

We knew that trainees would come up the drive with the baggage of bondage to sin, unforgiveness, and many differing wounds. Trainees would need to be healed and released from all that held them back from living the life God had planned. When NETS was finished it was our aim that they would go back down that drive in the freedom of Christ.

"'The harvest is plentiful," we kept quoting, "and we need to be about getting the labourers ready!" (See Matthew 9:37.) While the metaphors mixed farming and hospitals, we knew that we were living in a hurting world and Ellel Pierrepont had work to do.

Before we properly opened our doors for those first classes, with prayer as a foundation we recruited a ministry team and they all had their own Healing Retreat. We gave them some training but it was something of a fast-track in those days and everyone had to be a lead prayer minister.

## A SPECIAL MOMENT

One week before the doors opened, I was cleaning the window in the Great Hall when God suddenly spoke to me. He said, "This is one of My addresses. This is one of the places where I have put My Name and I have chosen to dwell."

Immediately I stopped what I was doing and just slid to the floor. For a moment I couldn't move. Everyone around gathered at my side and I attempted to explain what had just happened.

"The Lord spoke to me!" I exclaimed.

We prayed into what God had just said about Pierrepont being one of *His addresses*, and others confirmed it was the word of God for us. With thanksgiving, we acknowledged the provision of the Lord. Our Father had given us all we needed to provide a warm welcome to those who would, in obedience to the leading of the Lord Jesus Christ, come to learn from Him.

The Lord knew our hearts! He had given us the land, the buildings, the curriculum, the teachers and staff, and a precious prayer ministry team. Now, with trainees ready to start the very first NETS class, we had His blessing. *We had His blessing to begin NETS!*

## TEACHING NETS

My understanding was that Peter and his wife, Fiona,[4] would stay at Highfield, the headmaster's former house, for the first three months to bring the teaching. The Nine Week School at Glyndley Manor would form the core of our curriculum. I had done this course and had the notes from there. Peter had outlined the rest of the programme and since I thought he was going to teach it, I didn't concern myself too much with the details.

Peter came and taught on 'Foundations for the Healing Ministry' for the first week, which went really well. At the end of the week, he told me that he had to go back to Ellel Grange.

"How long will you be gone for?" I asked naively.

"I'm not sure but I'll certainly be back in July," was the reply!

There had obviously been some misunderstanding as to how much of NETS he was expecting to teach, and of course he was responsible for overseeing the whole of Ellel Ministries, not just Pierrepont.

At this point, I had only taught Healing Retreats and Healing Services. On team we had John Kilford, a retired Anglican vicar from Ellel Grange, who was willing to teach some subjects, and Fred Elgar, previously from Wholeness Through Christ, who was a good teacher. A number of visiting teachers were also available to come from Ellel Grange, but that was it. What was I going to do?

Have you ever had a mentor recognise you were ready to take on a task, before you had any idea you were ready and able to take it on? I felt like a baby eagle being tipped out of the nest, whose parent sees it is ready to fly. In my case, Peter saw I was ready to fly with the teaching on NETS. I now needed to accept what the Lord had told me in my original vision.

That day I had stood on a mosaic floor, in a room bereft of furnishings, stripped of everything of value, and in my hand had been a little pencil drawing on an envelope. I had held a mere sketch of the globe vision God had given me. Long before we had purchased Pierrepont, long before the prophecy of God providing every knife, spoon and fork, not to mention blue carpets, I had heard the word of the Lord speak to me, "I am asking *you* to lead the work here."

God's timing still amazes me.

I sat down and planned the next month ahead. This teaching would be the race I needed to run with perseverance (Hebrews 12: 1–2). God never said I had to be successful, but He asked me to be faithful.[5] I knew in my heart that from the day I had taken all of my certificates of achievement in sales and marketing to the dump, I had burnt my ploughshares. "The Holy Spirit will be your accreditation," I had heard God say to me. Now I needed the faith to believe that God had, indeed, called me to carry out this vision.

I set to work planning the teaching, every step of the way sensing what God had to say to me concerning what NETS trainees needed to hear, see and do. I taught on 'Freedom from Fear' all one day, and the next day did demonstration ministry with volunteer NETS trainees. To our everlasting gratitude, we saw God move.

The core of what I taught came from my own studies at the Ellel Ministries Nine Week School at Glyndley Manor, which consisted of material from the Modular School. The Modular School is a series of weekend courses where as much as possible is packed in, with five teaching sessions on the Saturday, starting at 9am, and Saturday night ministry continuing until 10pm. This concept of 9am to 10pm was carried over to NETS 1.

Peter did return, as well as Steve Hepden and Clive Corfield (who were teachers at Ellel Grange), to teach NETS trainees. I worked long hours to get the course established, and all the offices – including mine – were in the Cedars. Nicky Hemery was my PA and we managed the whole operation: finance, marketing, recruitment, banking and teaching. The ministry management was done by Ruth Dahl and Helen Kilford with covering support from Fiona Horrobin at Ellel Grange. On most days we worked till 10pm, with no day off. By the way, we had *no* money! Everything we had – and I mean absolutely everything – was given to us. Praise God for such generosity from His people.

With the classes, demonstration ministry and group work going on day and night for the first set of NETS trainees, in addition to running the continued refurbishment programme and training up a ministry team, it wasn't long before I said, "Thank heavens we have booked the Sandfords for two weeks."

By the time John and Paula Sandford[6] arrived, I was totally exhausted and needed some days off to recuperate. It was during this time that they took me to one side to say something that I was beginning to realise: that the concept of five sessions a day, six days a week, for six months was unsustainable. They suggested we start at 9.30am to give people a little more time in the mornings and to have from 12.45 till 2.45 for lunch. There needed to be two hours off in the middle of the day to enable people to do their washing, process the teaching, or just take a break – and we were not to allow any classes to extend into the evenings.

This was a radical change to the way we had all previously done it. With a full-time focus on getting the course off the ground, we were unable to make these daily schedule changes properly for NETS 1. At the end of NETS 1, there were a large number of really outstanding testimonies and lives changed, but they mostly went home on their knees! Still, we had got through our first NETS and we were able to implement this more balanced schedule from NETS 2 onward.

It is amazing how, as you walk in obedience to Him, God will birth into you His plan for your life. It may be a completely different set of circumstances to those you expected, but at the very back of your mind will come the thought, "I just think perhaps we can do it."

A growing confidence in His *complete plan for my life* was developing. At some time in the future, a time set only by God Himself, I want to hear those words, "Well done, good and faithful servant" (Matthew 25:21). Thankfully, it doesn't say "successful servant", it says "faithful servant". Again I was reminded that God doesn't require me to be successful, only to be faithful, and that was a great comfort.

# CULTURAL ADJUSTMENTS

As I looked at the trainees from many nations on those early NETS courses, I knew God had brought me to this particular ministry for the healing of the nations (Revelation 22:2). I had to teach that there is only one culture in which we are to adapt: the culture of the Kingdom of God. We find our own culture comfortable, but God is more interested in our spiritual growth than our comfort.

This cross-cultural aspect of God's Kingdom is central to all we do at Pierrepont. A key aspect of the teaching programme is to help trainees *adjust to each other,* as they learn the new freedom in Christ that crosses all cultural barriers.

God had prepared me for this aspect of our teaching on NETS. Years before, my father had been part of the British Army that liberated France from the Nazis. At his knee I had heard many times the story of how his troop had come into one French village, thirsty from walking mile upon mile. There in the village was a water pipe, but the pipe had a lock on it.

"One franc," said a local Frenchman.

89

"What?" said my father. "After all we have done for your nation, you would charge us a franc for a cup of water?"

"One franc," repeated the man from the village.

"I don't think so," said my father as he shot off the lock with his rifle.

The men had their fill of water that day, but my father never forgave that Frenchman. Years later, I was to hear him say, "Never trust someone from France or Germany. They always bring our country into their trouble. They cause trouble."

So when I was in prayer ministry training at Glyndley Manor, God in His wisdom had given me first a German person to pray for at a Healing Retreat, and then a French person in the second session. "God, what are You doing?" I asked.

Of course, God was showing me He was calling me to an international ministry and I could hold no prejudices. Prejudices must go! His word is for the healing of *all* nations.

Now, I needed not only to teach His word on NETS, but to help trainees from so many cultures to get along with each other as they gathered at Pierrepont. We can be neither Greek nor Jew nor Russian nor Ukrainian nor American nor English nor French, but one in Christ – and to God will be all the glory.

*Chapter Nine*

# Prayer for Healing

*… and healed those who needed healing*

(Luke 9:11)

In the early days, before Pierrepont opened its doors, many people came to Beryl Graham and myself for prayer. Far too many people came to us. We became exhausted with extremely long days of praying for people. That was why we organised the Farnham conference. Through conference teaching and prayer ministry, we could reach a greater number of people with God's word for healing. It was in preparation for this conference that we learned a key principle that would be taught at NETS.

We knew that in a group setting we could see more people come into the freedom of Christ, but first, God wanted to show us *how* He wanted us to pray for so many people at one time. With several hundred people booked to come to the Farnham conference, we realised we needed quite a number of prayer ministers. We needed people who would pray for those who, after receiving the teaching on healing and deliverance, would come up for prayer. Our priority was to find some prayer warriors who could help us teach new prayer ministers. Experienced prayer warriors, as we respectfully called Christian men and women who had spent years of searching the Scriptures and praying for the needs of others, would help us form a prayer ministry team. This team, in turn, would be equipped to pray for those who attended the conference.

## IONE AND STELLA

Beryl and I decided to visit two strong women of God in our community, Mrs Ione Carver and Dr Stella Walter.[1]

Ione and Stella were already on the journey of understanding the baptism of the Holy Spirit, and had been carrying out one-day healing events and even weekends in Ione's home. They led a young wives' prayer and Bible study group. They held weekend house parties totally dedicated to studying God's Word and praying for the needs of family and friends. We wanted their help.

Even before we arrived to meet and pray with Ione and Stella, a naval officer and his wife had said to Ione, "Did you know, people up north are teaching this stuff at some place called Ellel? What we need is a course to teach this to the churches down here in the south of England!"

So when we met to discuss the Farnham conference, Ione and Stella had already heard about Ellel and they had already experienced the reality that there were many hurting people, people in need of deep healing, in our communities. Once again we heard, from them, the words: "The harvest is plentiful but the workers are few" (Matthew 9:37). Thankfully, these two mature ladies were more than ready to help with the first Ellel healing conference in Farnham.

We needed to train as many people as possible to increase the workers in the field of the broken, the hurting and the wounded in a sin-sick world. Yet, we found quite a hurdle when it came to the fact that many, many long-term Christians lacked the confidence to step forward and simply pray according to the Scriptures for someone to be healed.

But as *every aspect* of the vision God had given was coming to fruition, He had a plan even for this hurdle – this challenge of bringing in workers.

(Dr) Stella Walter, part of that dynamic prayer duo, first presented a key to how we were to develop the prayer ministry team; it was originally for the Farnham conference, but it impacted the work that was ahead of us for Pierrepont itself. With her medical background, she had a question (or two!) that was to prove pivotal to giving the framework needed for many to step up to the faith required for the calling of prayer ministry.

## TEN MINUTES!!

While as a Christian doctor Stella believed God healed, she preferred to take *a considerable length of time* to make a thorough diagnosis, and then – only then – pray for the patient. Stella and Ione often took a day, or even days, to pray for those who came to them for prayer ministry.

Though Stella saw the need for healing prayers, and the growing interest from Christians to learn about the healing power of the Holy Spirit, she had some initial reservations about participating in our first conference. Her problem?

"What was the basis for this praying for healing at conferences or small ministry groups? How can a ministry team approach healing, in a biblical manner?" she asked herself, and she asked me.

The problem, the real hurdle in her thinking was – how could she be part of a prayer ministry team that simply prayed for someone for *ten minutes* at the end of a conference teaching session? How could we train Christian workers to do that?

As a doctor of medicine, Stella wanted to delve into symptoms and medical history, bringing her best medical assessment to the Lord. In her integrity, she was determined to pray the truth, and not simply what she thought was wrong with the person. She wanted to bring a diagnosis to the Lord for healing. What if the person coming forward for healing for an illness had no real idea what was wrong with them? Or what if they had been misdiagnosed?

To Stella's mind, simply taking a patient's word without diagnostics was no way to conduct a healing ministry! She and Ione were used to taking *at least* an entire day to pray for someone who was unwell, or battling a disease. What were we doing?

Stella's worries reflected the concerns of many. It all seemed too complicated.

Stella spent hours poring over the Scriptures to seek the will of the Lord in praying for healing, and sought the Lord deeply on this matter: "Lord, how do I pray for healing in this situation in a way that lines up with Your Word? We didn't learn this at medical school."

Then God showed her the scripture of Martha and Mary. The words leapt from the page!

> *"but only one thing is needed. Mary has chosen what is better, and it will not be taken away from her."*

> (Luke 10:42)

That was it! That was what she needed to hear from her Lord. As a Christian doctor she could go before the True Healer, the one who had died on the cross and whose stripes were all that were needed for healing, and she could pray, "Father, what is the one thing that is needful in this case, with this person, *at this time*?"

The Lord was the one who knew the diagnosis in its entirety, not Stella. He knew how she was to pray for that person who came forward for prayer. Stella's part would be, in each case, *to ask Him*.

Stella already believed that healing and deliverance was God's plan for His people. Through the laying on of hands and anointing with oil (whether someone was a trained doctor or not), He healed and delivered His people, through the blood of the Lord Jesus Christ.

The one thing that would always be needful was to sit at the feet of her Lord, and ask Him, "Lord, for this person who has come for prayer ministry, how would You like me to pray at this time?"

As the Farnham conference got underway, and the teaching in the school auditorium began, Stella was given a prayer partner to assist her. Groups of prayer ministers stood two by two as the people came forward for prayer. Stella and her assistant prayer minister waited as their first 'patient' approached.

Graciously, the Lord reinforced what He had said in the Scriptures. Stella's prayer partner confessed that she knew much less than Stella about praying for the sick and that she was scared.

"I don't really know how to pray for anyone who is sick or in some need," said the new prayer minister.

"Don't you worry," replied Stella. "The Lord has already told me we are to pray to Him, and ask Him, 'Lord, what is the one thing needed?' We'll wait on Him and He will tell us."

And the new prayer minister was excited to discover that the Lord led them as He had promised. People still come to me today with stories of what God did for them at that weekend in Farnham!

Today, in their eighties and nineties, Stella and Ione are both still going strong in the Lord. They are a vital part of Pierrepont's teaching and prayer ministry team, which includes participating in a number of Healing Retreats.

## HEALING RETREATS

Healing Retreats are an integral part of what we do in Ellel Ministries. Up to thirty people attend for two days and they share in times of worship and teaching. In addition, each person is offered personal prayer ministry in a safe and loving environment. Healing Retreats usually last from Tuesday evening until Thursday afternoon, although we sometimes have one-day retreats as well. Some are specifically for church leaders. There is no charge for a Healing Retreat; they are funded through donations and sometimes by God's miraculous supply (see chapter eleven for examples).

We encourage all our prayer ministers to ask the same question that Stella asked: "What is the one special thing that God wants to do on this retreat?" Every time, there are many testimonies of God's healing love impacting people.

## PAT'S STORY

One part of the Healing Retreat teaching is looking at what the Scriptures teach about the importance of forgiveness. This is a true story we shared with the first NETS trainees:

Pat was a lady who came to one of the first Healing Retreats at Ellel Grange. She came because she had a longstanding problem with pain in her back, and had to wear a large brace for support. Peter Horrobin was teaching on the first evening and he concluded his talk by mentioning the importance of forgiveness, which is a major key to healing. He asked the guests to spend some time that evening making a list of people they needed to forgive.

Pat was furious.

"How dare Peter Horrobin tell me to forgive? He doesn't know what these people did to me! Besides, I've been bitter for thirty years and if I forgive them now, I will have wasted all those years. How dare he?"

She was so annoyed that she decided she had had enough of this. Instead of staying for the retreat, she packed her case, got into her car and drove home – two hours driving in the dark and rain. Once at home, she took herself to bed, still angry.

But she couldn't sleep.

And she still couldn't sleep.

At four o'clock in the morning, she sat up in bed and said to God, "All right, You win!", and wrote out a list which she entitled 'My hate list'.

Pat then prayed through the list of people she had hated for thirty years and she made a choice to forgive them. After that she lay down and was able to sleep.

In the morning, she was woken up by the sound of ticking from her alarm clock. This may not sound unusual, but it was for Pat, because she was completely deaf in one ear and 80 per cent deaf in the other ear. She wore hearing aids, which of course she took out at night to sleep.

God had miraculously healed her overnight. She could hear!

Well, of course she came rushing back to Ellel Grange to tell everyone. Further prayer during the retreat resulted in healing to her back as well. Hallelujah!

God had been waiting to bless her, but she had been blocking His healing by her unforgiveness. Pat is not the only one to have experienced physical healing after forgiving; there are many others. I am not saying that healing is always simple and straightforward, but forgiveness of those who have hurt us (or those we love) is key to any healing.

Forgiveness is not just someone's good idea; it is God's Kingdom truth, the way His Kingdom works. Forgiveness really is the gateway to healing.[2] Forgiveness is a transaction between us and God, rather than a transaction between us and the person who hurt us. We choose to forgive from our heart in agreement with the Word of God. Only then can He give us the spiritual empowerment to forgive those people who have done us wrong, who have hurt and wounded our spirit, soul or body (1 Thessalonians 5:23).

As we teach about healing, we are teaching from the Word of God. There are many more keys to healing in God's Word. Our textbook must be the Holy Word, the Scriptures. Everything we teach at a conference or in a classroom must line up with that Word. Luke 9:1–2 reads, "Then He [Jesus] called His twelve disciples together and gave them power and authority over all demons, and to cure diseases. He sent them to preach the kingdom of God and to heal the sick" (NKJV). The more we apply the principles of the Kingdom of God in our lives, the more healing we will see.

# QUESTIONS

But if we are honest, most of us have quite big questions about prayer for healing. Ellel Ministries doesn't teach that we are to 'name it and claim it' when it comes to healing. We acknowledge the sovereignty of God and the need to discern the work of the Holy Spirit. It is *His* power that brings healing. We must ask Him what *He* is doing at this time in this person's life.

Yet many of us find it difficult to pray for someone's healing. We think it is something that 'somebody else' should do, 'not me'.

So we need to look at the reality of our problems with prayer. That is key to our curriculum on the NETS course. Prayer plays an essential part in the Kingdom of our Lord Jesus Christ.

God can say "Yes" to our prayers and God can say "No". Yet, that famous Methodist evangelist John Wesley said, "God does nothing on the earth save in answer to believing prayer."

My challenge to our NETS groups is: Does a sovereign, all-powerful God need our involvement or not?

God is complete. God is perfect. God is Almighty. God is all-knowing. God can be in all places at once.

Does God really need us? Does He require our input?

If we come to the conclusion that "No, He doesn't need us", then prayer can't be necessary. We could think, "God is just going to do what He is going to do. He is Almighty, so why bother to pray?"

I am sure God can cope with such big questions from us.

In some places around the world we hear teaching that our all-powerful God doesn't need anything, including our prayers. We can also hear teaching that says all we need to do is *tell* God that we claim our healing. I don't believe that either of these represents properly what the Bible teaches about prayer.

Because God is Almighty, He could do whatever He chose without us; but *He has chosen* the dynamic of prayer. This is an amazing privilege. He has given us the privilege of moving the hands of God, changing the things we pray for, because we pray. Often we can find that God is limiting Himself; not to rescue, not to save, not to do it, unless somebody stands in the gap and prays (Ezekiel 22:30). He often chooses to limit or hold back His blessing if we choose not to be obedient to His way of living. Often we miss the little word "if" in God's promises of blessings.

2 Chronicles 7:14 says "*if* my people, who are called by my name, will humble themselves and pray and seek my face and turn from their wicked ways, *then* will I hear from heaven and will forgive their sin and will heal their land" (my italics).

There are a lot more "if/then" statements in the Bible than we sometimes realise.[3] This came as a blinding revelation to me, and I have been a Christian since I was thirteen.

Yet, even if we know that prayer does change things, we must still answer the question central to all these questions, that key question of: "Can *my* prayer change things?"

# ROS' STORY

Ros is someone who had questions about whether God would really use her, but as she allowed the Lord to touch her own life, she discovered that the doors opened before her. This is what she wrote to us:

My husband Al and I did stages 1 and 2 of NETS in 2009/10. It was, and remains, the most significant, precious and wonderful period of our entire lives and we are still experiencing the huge benefits and blessings we received from being at Pierrepont for those months.

We were more 'senior' members of the large group, and the diversity of the group was extraordinary, but all one in Christ Jesus. For me it was a foretaste of heaven.

We came (our agenda) to be trained to 'do' healing prayer ministry, yet throughout the course we didn't number ourselves among those whose gifting was so obvious. We both experienced the blessing of healing of our own past hurts and trauma.

On our return to Australia, grieving for the life we had left behind, we were confronted with family tragedy and were and still are committed to supporting the shocked and grieving. All we had gained really helped to prepare us for this time.

I wondered if I would ever get to be involved in healing prayer ministry. However, the Lord's timing is perfect and I am now a member of Sonrise Family Ministries. I was reluctant at first but was encouraged by the leadership there and it has now become a blessing and a joy to see the way the Lord so graciously chooses to work through us to bring His blessing, healing, deliverance and comfort to those who come for ministry. I am overwhelmed by the privilege.

I would also like to praise and thank God for a miraculous physical healing I received. One day, the teacher (Ruth Hawkey) said she sensed the Lord wanted to do some physical healing, so would we all put our hands on the part of our body we would like Him to heal. I had a hand condition which was troubling me at that time, so I put my hands together. At the end of the prayer my hands remained unchanged, but something else happened. I had been experiencing terrible pain in my knees for a long time and one of my knees kept slipping out of joint.

From that day to this, I have had no trouble with my knees at all.

NETS can stand for Never Ever The Same. I didn't feel the difference immediately but the spiritual development that has taken place in my life since is where I see the long-term effects of the time we spent at Pierrepont.

# SENT BY GOD

I believe that as we respond to God's word in our own lives, as Ros did, He will indeed use us. We don't have to be someone 'special' for God to hear our prayers. It is His work, not ours. It is His Kingdom. As disciples of Jesus, we are to be representatives of God's Kingdom; we are workers for the Lord Jesus Christ. He wants to heal people.

In my career when I started off in sales, I was called a 'representative' of the business. I didn't make the goods, so I was not the manufacturer or the designer; I simply represented the company to the person who was going to purchase the goods.

If someone asks us why we are doing what we are doing at Pierrepont, the answer is that "The Lord Jesus Christ has sent us". The only authority we have in this healing and deliverance ministry is the authority of the Lord Jesus Christ, who said, "I have given you authority … to overcome all the power of the enemy" (Luke 10:19). Jesus is the Redeemer; we are the releasers of His work. This is our qualification to proclaim the gospel, to heal the sick, to cast out demons and proclaim the second coming of Jesus.

This is not our good idea. It cannot be our good idea; we are sent by God. *He* commissions *us*. God sent His only begotten Son into the world. Then Jesus, having done that finished work on the cross, said, "I am sending you."

God is calling us to see the needs of people and to intercede, to stand in the gap. *God wants to hear our prayers.* He wants us to call out to Him. The apostle James said: "You do not have, because you do not ask God" (James 4:2).

## USING TIME WISELY

We cannot go around in spiritual neutral gear. We must not waste our time. I encourage people who come to Pierrepont to pray as they walk down to Cedars for a meal. Whatever we are doing, whether it is cleaning, walking by the river that flows across our base, or clearing the grounds, we can pray. Pray over the food, pray over the beds, pray over the teaching, pray over the Healing Retreats. Of course, corporate prayer is important but we need to be people of prayer. We need the power of God to be released in these thirty-five acres, for His glory to come down in a fresh way.

Jesus often withdrew to a solitary place and prayed. We come around the communion table each Friday morning at Pierrepont, and we pray too. We pray that God will call people to leave behind their homes or jobs to come to Pierrepont for training and spend time in His Word and at His feet. We pray Jesus will prompt us all to pray more than we do, to draw aside and to seek His face, to know His will. And we pray that Jesus will come and profoundly put into all of our belief systems that we have been sent by the Lord Jesus Christ to proclaim the Kingdom truth, to heal the sick in spirit, soul and body.

*Chapter Ten*

# Deliverance

*... deliver us from evil: For thine is the kingdom, and the power,
and the glory, for ever*

(Matthew 6:13, KJV)

Around 2005 I flew to Bangkok, Thailand, where we intended to
hold an Ellel Ministries conference. The evening before I was due to
teach, the vicar of the church wanted to have a word with me.

"I'm not happy about you teaching on the subject of deliverance,"
said the vicar. "I would prefer you didn't mention it."

Having come a very long way from England to Thailand to
teach *precisely on healing and deliverance*, I wasn't sure what to say
to him. After a moment or two of reflection, I said I would consider
what to do and get back to him the next day. I started praying!

I am a visual person, so as I prayed I asked God to give me
something visual, an illustration I could use to explain to the vicar
what I wanted to teach.

## A HOUSE WITH FOUR DOORS

That night God gave me a picture of a house with four doors. The
house represented our lives, for the Bible says our bodies are a temple
of the Holy Spirit (1 Corinthians 6:19–20).

Each door in this house represented one of the main ways the enemy can gain a foothold in our lives. On the NETS course, we teach from the Bible about the ways in which the enemy gains rights to influence our lives.

I made PowerPoint slides showing the house with its doors. The first slide showed the house with a skull and crossbones flag at the top, depicting it as under the management of the enemy.

When we become Christians we have a new owner; we are 'under new management' because on the cross Christ paid the price for our lives. So on the next slide I showed a new flag on top of the house, which said 'Jesus is Lord'. This is to demonstrate that when we become Christians, we become Christ's rich possession. A Christian is not 'possessed' by a demon.[1]

I showed these slides to the vicar and explained that although Jesus is the new owner of the house, any intruders which had already entered through the open doors may still be present. There will still be a need to remove any intruders and to clean up the house. A demon that came in through one of these doors before a person was saved does not automatically leave when the person gets saved; in fact, they will try to hang on to their place.

In the early Church, when a person came out of paganism to Christianity, they were delivered of their demons before baptism as a believer. Getting rid of the enemy is simply a part of declaring that Jesus, not Satan, is Lord of our lives. Learning to live under this 'new management' is all part and parcel of discipleship. James 4:7 tells us "Resist the devil, and he will flee from you".

Clearly, as well as evicting the enemy, we must 'close the doors', which means dealing with the underlying footholds, the reasons why the enemy was able to get in. Issues such as sin are like open doors and will give the enemy ongoing rights to influence a person's life. If the enemy is evicted, but such 'doors' are not closed, he can return. Jesus warned us about this in Luke 11:24–26. Jesus must be Lord of the house, which is why anyone in need of deliverance must either be a Christian or quickly become a Christian.

One aspect of this teaching that becomes more obvious when using the house illustration is that even when someone becomes a Christian and is 'under new management' they still have work to do to clean up the house. When the enemy has been living in the house, there will be damage to repair afterwards.

I believe the best preparation for deliverance is to remove the rights the enemy has to be in a person's life. It is a good description of what God does in the lives of people who come to Ellel Ministries.

The enemy gets rights from things such as sin we have not repented of, or our wrongful responses to wounding. After the open doors of sin and wounding are shut, through repentance and healing, the rights the enemy has to be there are removed. Deliverance is then straightforward; it becomes a natural consequence. All this happens only through the blood of Jesus, by His finished work on the cross. We need to learn how to keep doors shut to the enemy – with our new life in Christ. Ephesians 4:27 says we are to give no place to the devil.

I had another meeting with the vicar to explain this illustration of the house that God had shown me, and he was certainly "happier than he had been" and he allowed us to go ahead. We had a good time in that particular church and God moved in healing and deliverance. The vicar himself was busy and did not attend many of our meetings, and finally the time came for us to leave. We wondered what the long-term results would be of our teaching.

Many years later, a lady came to his church who was very troubled – she had become a Christian but had started to strongly manifest evil spirits and shout out in the services. The vicar finally spoke to his bishop in Singapore, and mentioned that the only ministry he knew of that could deal with such things was Ellel Ministries in England. "Well, that's very interesting," said the bishop, "because one of my vicars in Singapore is also the director of Ellel Ministries in Singapore! I will ask him and his wife to fly out to Bangkok to pray with your lady."

Esther and Titus Soo, the directors of Ellel Ministries in Singapore, who had previously done NETS, duly flew out to Bangkok and were booked into a hotel for three nights to spend time with this very troubled lady. However, in two sessions the lady was completely delivered and had been brought into much inner healing as well. So after only one night's stay in the hotel, Esther and Titus were able to fly back to Singapore. And so it was I felt that God had honoured us pushing through, back in 2005, over the question of deliverance.

## MAKE DISCIPLES

Recently, one of our teachers asked a room of thirty-two Christians if any of them came from a church that dealt with or taught on issues of deliverance. Only five raised their hands. It is a subject we often skirt around, yet it is mentioned many times in the Bible.

Jesus says that He came to proclaim liberty to the captives and of sight to the blind, to set at liberty those who are oppressed, taking back what the enemy has stolen (Luke 4:17–19, Isaiah 61:1, John 10:10). Adam left the garden after succumbing to temptation. Now Jesus, the second Adam, makes a way for us to come back into a direct, loving relationship with the Father (Romans 5:12–21, 1 Corinthians 15:45).

I came to Christ through the Billy Graham crusade, and I believe the work of the evangelist has been carried out to an excellent standard in many parts of the world. Yet, even the Billy Graham team says that new believers can fall away after they commit their lives to Christ if there is no follow-up to support them in the local church.[2] I believe one of the greatest needs in this world is not necessarily for more evangelists, though that is an excellent calling, but for disciple-makers, who as shepherds will heal and train the flock. We need people who are willing to help with this vital work, which must include removing the rights of the enemy in the lives of ordinary men and women.

The world and the media often like to talk about deliverance in terms of the word 'possession'. They depict deliverance as like something from the film *The Exorcist*, and quite scary. The enemy's best tactic to keep Christians from dealing with this issue is fear and distraction. We are often just too busy to deal with the pressing issues in our hearts, and Satan wants us to believe that this topic is way beyond what the normal person is able to deal with. The enemy often makes himself look as if he is more powerful than he actually is.

When the rights of the enemy have been removed, deliverance is a gentle process that can be carried out in love with godly authority.[3] That is why it is so important to teach people first, so that they can deal with the footholds that the enemy is holding on to in their lives. Once these rights are removed, it is so much easier to evict the intruders. And the testimonies of changed lives are awe-inspiring. Our God is a mighty and deeply loving Healer, who longs to rescue His people and set captives free.[4]

*Chapter Eleven*

# Lifting the Bowls

*Then you will know which way to go, since you have never been this way before*

(Joshua 3:4)

A few years ago we needed £10,000, and we needed it just before Christmas. We got to the last working day before the deadline of needing that money, and I called the team together. I said, "Can we pray for this £10,000? It needs to come today!"

And so we stood and prayed, "Lord, here's our bowl… and we just hand it up to You and say 'Would You come and fill up our bowl with the £10,000 that we need?'"

We finished praying that morning and went into the day. I would see the team again at lunch, which was our last meal together before the Christmas break. In the office I carried on with my work and looked again at the post. There were a few Christmas cards – but none with a much-needed cheque.

At the end of the morning I went down the steps of the staircase by the Great Hall, ready to head out of the door to lunch, quite sad that we had not had our prayer answered. I now had to face the team and I thought, "Well, I'm not going to have a very nice Christmas worrying about this."

As I was walking down the steps, I heard the Post Office van pulling up outside. I saw there was a second delivery, which we never have, except occasionally at Christmas. The postman stopped and put one envelope into my hand, with my name on it. He hurriedly drove off, and I opened the envelope. There was no letter inside, no Christmas card, but there was a money order for – guess what – £10,000!

I rushed straight down to the team and handed the cheque around.

People were stunned. Who would give this kind of money to *us*?

One or two South Africans started to convert it to Rand, which came to a very large number!

We were all amazed, joyfully giving thanks.

What a faithful, wonderful God!

You know, God has taken me in steps from one level to another when it comes to understanding His financial provision. That is the way He teaches me, as I continue learning to trust Him for all we need. I had never walked this way before, this road of financing a ministry that is by Him and for Him.

## A CAR PARK

So at this point I had seen the hand of God provide every knife, fork and spoon; all the material goods we wanted – and even items we didn't necessarily *want*, but the local council said we must have. For example, two years after we purchased Pierrepont, the Waverley Borough Council insisted that we must have a large car park on site. When it was a school, there had only been a few car parking spaces outside the main house, but the council wanted us to have at least thirty car parking spaces available for people coming on courses.

We allocated a field next to the headmaster's former house (Highfield), and with our own team we dug out the footings and sold the topsoil from this area to our architect. Then our grounds manager, Paul Graham, noticed a farm that he passed each day on his way to work at Pierrepont. The farm had a huge heap of rocks outside. One day Paul felt prompted by the Lord to go and knock on the farmer's door and ask him what he was going to do with the rocks, which seemingly had lain there for ages. The farmer replied that he had bought them to make a road up to his farmhouse but he was now moving. We could have them for free if we paid to have them transported away.

With the money we received from selling the topsoil, we paid for the trucks to transport this huge amount of rock back to Pierrepont. It was hard work laying these on the footings, but when we finished we had exactly the right amount of rock! We now needed a topping for the car park, but we couldn't afford it, so someone had the brainwave of ringing Surrey County Council to enquire whether they were resurfacing the road anywhere near us. The reply was that just up the road at Churt (approximately two miles away) they were doing road repairs and had tarmac scrapings available at £1 a tonne! Two members of our team went up to negotiate, and arranged for Surrey County Council vehicles to transport the tarmac to our car park.

Again, it was a lot of hard work levelling this tarmac out, and then we needed their steamroller! Our men returned to negotiate again, and arranged for a steamroller to come by and roll out the car park. We ended up with a thirty- to forty-space car park for less than £200. The Waverley council inspectors came and said our car park was much higher quality than we would have had from a domestic company because it was road-quality tarmac. Once again, we stood amazed at how the Lord had worked things out in our favour.

## THE BUSH HOTEL

We have seen His provision in so many shapes and forms, often in surprising ways, and there are just so many people to thank and to appreciate for their generous contribution to making Pierrepont the warm and welcoming house it has become.

One day I had a phone call from Mike Maybury, a team member, saying that the Bush Hotel in Farnham had contacted him. They were refurbishing and had a number of good-quality chairs and sofas they no longer needed. They wondered whether Pierrepont might be interested in them for the small price of £100. Of course, I said, "Yes, please." Mike went to collect them and they asked him if he wanted the curtains too. These were lying in a heap, having just been taken down, so he picked them up as well.

The Long Room at Pierrepont (now the library) was very much in need of some curtains and, would you believe it, they were perfect. Exactly the right colour in burgundy and cream to match the carpet; exactly the right number for the number of windows, and most amazingly of all, exactly the right size! There were five different-sized windows in the room and each one had its match. There was even one set of these lovely, expensive curtains which exactly fitted the large bay window at the end of the room with its long drop. Not one pin or stitch had to be put in them and they adorned the whole room beautifully.

## £50,000

There is nothing like a financial need when it comes to testing where your focus of attention lies, and soon God took us up another step-level in learning to trust for His financial provision. Running Pierrepont costs a lot of money, with large numbers of trainees and staff to accommodate, feed and keep warm, as well as meeting our responsibility of large monthly payments to the bank for the mortgage. Sometimes bills arrive all at once.

One of the most challenging lessons took place while I was in Malacca, Malaysia, teaching at a prayer ministry school. In the midst of trying to concentrate on the teaching, I was receiving a deluge of emails from Pierrepont saying, "We need a lot of money. A lot of money this time. £50,000!"

It was urgent. We needed the money immediately.

At the end of my teaching, when I was ready to fly back home, I printed off my emails at the hotel where I had been staying. I stuffed them into my carry-on bag to read later during the flight back to the UK. (This was a time before you could read your emails on your phone!)

Before boarding the Singapore-London flight, I checked once again that the pile of printed-out emails was in my hand luggage. When on the plane, I pulled out those pieces of paper, one after the other. Each email sounded more urgent than the one before; we needed this money to keep Pierrepont running.

You know how little room you have when you are in an economy seat? Especially when the person in the seat in front of you reclines theirs? Overwhelmed by the urgency and the amount of our financial need, I just dropped on to my knees right there in the footwell of this economy seat and started to cry out: "Oh God, don't ask me to carry on leading Pierrepont without this £50,000 that I haven't got. I can't do it. Oh God, I can't carry on like this. Please hear my cry. Oh God, I am really banging on the gates of heaven for this. Please give us this £50,000!"

I could feel the anointing of the Holy Spirit as I prayed.

Then God said to me, "Get up. Get off your knees and sit down. It's done!"

How would you feel? What would you do?

I was travelling with Sharon Chong, a lady from the Pierrepont team, and I turned to her and said, "God is telling me this £50,000 is done in the heavenly realm. What's on the movies?"

When I finally arrived home after the all-night flight, I got in through the front door of my house, picked up the phone in the hall and rang the accountant at Pierrepont. I said, "I got all your emails about the problems we have. Just give me an update."

He was a bit quiet on the other end of the phone. "Guess what? Someone has *just* come into the office with a cheque for £50,000!" So our prayers went from £10,000 to £50,000.

## NEXT STEP

Then in 2007 we needed money to clear a lot of financial commitments and for a number of projects we felt the Lord was leading us to do, for which we had no funds. At a leadership meeting I asked, "When it is all added up, how much do we need?"

"£200,000," said a member of the leadership team.

It's getting a bit more desperate now, isn't it?

I said, "OK, who has got the faith to pray and stand with me and ask God for £200,000?"

They all said, "Yes, God can do it."

We started to *cry out to God* and to pray. We had a time of spiritual warfare as we fought the enemy, saying, "Get your foot off our supply line!"

"We release those funds," we declared. I said, "I speak to the north and the south and the west and the east – release the funds that we need in this ministry!"

But though we prayed, nothing seemed to happen. A week went by, and still nothing happened. No cheque in the post. No one just walked into the finance office and produced a money order.

The ministry manager at that time was an American lady named Joyce Romack. She was known for her exuberant "Hallelujah!"s during services and sermons. She came to me and said, "Jill, I believe we should take up an offering at our communion services each Friday."

I said, "Well, it's a bit difficult, as we haven't been able to pay the staff for a while. Is it right to say to them 'Would you like to give?' when they haven't been paid?" But Joyce felt this idea, of an offering given by all who attended communion on Fridays at Pierrepont, was an idea from God. She persisted, so I said to the team, "OK... we are going to have a heap offering. I want everybody to bring something. God doesn't ask you to bring what you don't have. Just bring *something*; bring anything that you can bring."

While we took the offering, what I especially remember from that service was saying to Jilly Lyon-Taylor, a member of our leadership team, "Look how people are coming out with absolute smiles on their faces!" We had an amazing time; what I can only call a "triumphant time of praise and worship, singing glory to God".

Afterwards, almost overwhelmed by the joy of the service, the leadership team and I went upstairs into our usual Friday leaders' meeting. We attended to the agenda for that day and had a lot to discuss.

Now, there was a young woman who worked in the finance office. Her name was Aurora and she was Spanish. Suddenly, Aurora rushed up into the leaders' meeting, very excited, and said, "Somebody put a note in the communion offering, promising to give £220,000!"

And one of the leaders said, "No, Aurora dear, you probably mean £22,000. Maybe a misunderstanding between the languages."

"No, no, no!" Aurora insisted she had the correct figure.

Jilly Lyon-Taylor asked her to write down the number she was trying to say, but I knew there was only one way to be sure – I told Aurora to bring the note to us.

She brought it and someone had indeed put a note in the offering plate during communion, for £220,000.

Oh Lord, this is truly amazing!

## THE NEHEMIAH LESSON

Pushing through takes a lot of tenacity. In building this major project for the Lord, I have been particularly impacted by the perseverance, the tenacity, the ability to push through, of Nehemiah. The people faced huge opposition in rebuilding Jerusalem. The enemies Sanballat, Tobiah and Geshem showed up very quickly as Nehemiah got going on all he was called to do for God (Nehemiah 6:1).

Is it going to be any different for us in building this ministry at Pierrepont? Will it be any different for you in what God calls you to do for Him? I don't think so. I have always found it amazing that people came to Nehemiah and told him "*ten times* over" (Nehemiah 4:12, my italics), "It will never happen. God will never give you enough money. The workers are tired, discouraged."

Nobody said this work we are doing was going to be easy. We are doing a major work for the Lord. We must be careful we aren't "living next to the enemy", that we are not listening all the time to negative things. Perseverance is part of the fruit of the Spirit. In fact, if we were unopposed in what we were doing for God, I would be inclined to stop and ask, "Are we building the right wall?"

In Pierrepont's story, there were plenty of people who came and said to me, "Are you kidding? This derelict place? You only have a few feeble workers. This place is a bankrupt school. It's been stripped of everything. You don't have any money. This isn't going to fly." And they walked away.

But we kept building the wall, so to speak, as we built up the ministry and refurbished the buildings. We kept trusting God, and are still trusting God, to fulfil the vision; to bring representatives from all countries and nations to Pierrepont to be trained and equipped. When we are building for God, it must be in all our hearts to finish the vision God gave us.

It is so important we understand the corporate nature of this building work. Nehemiah could not build the wall on his own and neither can we. We are all part of the body of Christ. Pierrepont is part of Ellel Ministries, a family of nearly thirty centres worldwide, all supporting one another. At Pierrepont itself we currently have nine leaders, and there are about sixty team members. Everyone plays their part, both individually and as a team. As on any team, there are strengths and weaknesses, and as the director of Pierrepont I continually seek the Lord as to how to guide the leadership and the team as a whole and, of course, we pray regularly together.

Nehemiah prayed seventeen times, but he also said the workers were to go to the lowest places (the vulnerable spots), and a trumpet would blow if there was a problem, so that they could gather together to defend what was being built.

What is the modern equivalent of blowing the trumpet? Mobile phones, emails, tweets, prayer requests? We blow the modern trumpet. As we do this work for God we know our strengths, but we must also be aware of our weak areas, our exposed places. Like Nehemiah, we must station people at the lowest places of the wall.

As we grow in strength and numbers, offering more and more to a hurting and broken world, equipping the Church for His Kingdom living, the opposition increases its efforts to stop what we are doing. It isn't just the economy, or a world increasingly resistant to the Christian message. We need to expect Sanballat, Tobiah, and Geshem as well, understanding the strategies Satan uses to oppose the people of God. Nehemiah called in the troops and acted wisely. What they were doing, what they were building, had to be their complete focus.

Nehemiah's workers couldn't spread themselves too thinly around the wall, and we mustn't spread ourselves too thinly. We need to have each other in sight, and I have challenged myself to keep a humility that allows me to blow the trumpet when we are in trouble and not to think we can do this work on our own. "God opposes the proud but gives grace to the humble" (James 4:6).

## THE 20p LESSON

The Lord has taught me in so many ways. One lesson came as I was driving home from doing some shopping in Farnham. It was raining heavily, and suddenly the car began to make a strange sound. I didn't have a phone with me, or a raincoat, not expecting to be out in the rain for any length of time. The car suddenly stopped.

It just stopped.

I looked ahead and saw a red telephone box down the road. Quickly getting out of the car and locking the door, I started to run to the phone box. I realised it was further away than I anticipated, so I got very puffed out and very, very wet. I finally arrived. At least I was getting out of the rain!

Everything was soaking, my hair streaming with water. I looked hastily in my purse for the required 20p coin, but there were only a few pennies and a £5 note. I needed a 20p coin for the phone in the telephone box to work, to call Pierrepont to ask someone to come and get me.

No 20p coin to make the phone call! "Lord, I can't be doing with this right now!"

And God spoke to me. Often you know it's God when you don't want to hear it. *My car has broken down. I am wet through. I need to get hold of someone at Pierrepont, and God is trying to say something.*

He said to me, "You need a 20p piece."

"Yes, Lord, I need a 20p piece. I know!"

"And you've only got a £5 note."

"Yes, Lord, I've only got a £5 note."

God said to me, "Sometimes I need a 20p piece. Do you *have* to be a £5 note all the time? Sometimes a £5 note doesn't work – like now. Sometimes a £5 note is pretty useless, and I need a 20p piece."

I knew God was speaking to me. Maybe God was starting to deal with that bit of pride. It is so easy for me to be the upfront person, a leader, high-profile. But actually God was saying to me, are you willing to be a 20p piece when I need one?

So there in the phone box, with my mascara running down my face, my hair dripping, I prayed to the Lord, "Oh Lord, I repent of any pride in me that only wants to be a £5 note, and I freshly surrender,

Lord Jesus, to You… that whenever You want me to be a 20p piece I will be available as a 20p piece."

I knew it was an important time with the Lord, even if it was terribly inconvenient. As I looked down through my tears, suddenly there in the coin box was a 20p piece. Who put that there? Presumably the previous person; perhaps their call hadn't connected and their money went into the returned coin box. Do you believe in God's miraculous provision, when we truly trust Him by faith? I was able to make my call and get help.

The important thing on my agenda was for me to get help for me and my car, but His agenda was to get me to that place where I could say, "Yes, Lord, I am willing to be a 20p piece for You whenever You need one."

## THE JAM JAR METHOD

When I was a young person, my mother sat me down and taught me how to budget wisely. She taught me the jam jar method. It was a very good system, actually, especially as we used cash in those days.

I had to put money into one jar for the things I had to pay out; then I had a savings jar, a giving-at-church jar, a spending jar and a holiday jar. When I got married I carried on with the jam jar system. I put the money for taxes in one jar, the rent money in another jar, and the good news was that when those bills came, the money was there in the jars.

I may have started to learn about money in quite a juvenile way, but it actually worked. I didn't just come to church on Sunday and think, "Oh, what's in my pocket?" and give that. I had thought about tithing. I thought about having the money ready to give.

I believe we need to look at how we manage our money as Kingdom people. It is good to budget and to spend only what we can afford.

Paul says to Timothy, "Make sure the elders can manage well" (see 1 Timothy 3:4). An elder's family and their affairs need to be especially well-managed. Why should God trust us with Kingdom money if we can't manage our personal money?

Are we content with God's provision?

It's a question I have to ask myself, too. I love a bargain as much as the next person. I remember watching television years ago with my late husband, Ron, when we saw an advertisement for a bread-making machine.

"I must have one!" I said, delighted at this time-saving device.

Ron said, "*Must* have one? Five minutes ago you didn't even know it existed, and now you *must* have it?"

He was right.

One of the greatest challenges in leading a large and growing ministry is discerning just how God wants us to proceed with finances (or anything else, for that matter) at any given time. I have always wanted His clear direction.

We need to ask ourselves, "Is this a time, O Lord, when You are asking me to step out first and then Your provision will follow? Is this a 'River Jordan' moment (Joshua 3:14–17)? Or is this a time, O Lord, when I must wait for You to act before I make a move? Is this a 'Pillar of Cloud by Day and Pillar of Fire by Night' season (Exodus 13:20–22, Exodus 40:36–38)?"

I must have total trust in His direction, knowing His arm is never too short (Isaiah 59:1) and that He always pays for what He orders. There is nothing like a trial, a challenge, to know what our faith is made of, and "the testing of [our] faith produces endurance"(James 1:3, CEB). It produces the ability to bear up and wait on the Lord for His direction, including His financial direction. This type of endurance must have its maturing result (James 1:4).

This trust for our financial need is a continuing process, as trust grows through experience with God. This maturing of our faith is not just for those who founded Ellel Ministries, nor solely for those of us who developed Peter's vision for Pierrepont. It is for everyone involved. Even after buildings have been refurbished, bedrooms decorated and ministry teams established, we still need a mature faith for His provision. For all of us, those who have been here from the beginning of this ministry to the newest arrival on team, it is an act of faith to "lift our bowls" for His provision.

For example, on 10 January 2011 we were praying for a blessing for Cedars, our restaurant. That same week, our oven, gas cooker and fridge all broke! Now this was a serious problem. We feed many people as they come to conferences or Healing Retreats, as well as NETS trainees and team. In faith, we knew that God was going to do something great.

When we researched the cost of an oven, we found that the Rational oven we needed was £13,890 and in addition we had to meet a health and safety regulation for a new ventilation system for the Cedars' kitchen. The ventilation system, on its own, would cost another £13,000. These costs would be on top of the money needed for a gas cooker and a fridge.

Faith is built on the experience of trust as we follow the Lord. It does not mean that we take God's provision for granted. But it does mean there can be a certain expectation, a certain wonder at just *how* God will provide – *this time*.

Within days Pierrepont was blessed with the money for the new kitchen equipment, including the new ventilation system. The donor does not wish to be honoured and thanked for this gift, but we continue to give thanks and acknowledge that God is our provider. He is good all the time, every time.

On Thursday, 7 April 2011, the new Rational oven was installed. The next day the Pierrepont leaders came after communion and prayed for the Cedars' kitchen, anointing all the new equipment with oil. There before us was the evidence of His provision: a new cooker, oven, dishwasher and fridge, and a ventilation system.

God is establishing the work of our hands, as we endeavour to give a warm and hospitable welcome to those who come to Pierrepont. Our cup overflows!

*Chapter Twelve*

# Blessed Are the Flexible!

*... From everyone who has been given much, much will be demanded; and from the one who has been entrusted with much, much more will be asked*

(Luke 12:48)

Peter's original vision for NETS had been for a one-year course. In 1996 we began with six months – Stages One and Two[1] – but by summer 2000 it was time to expand. What should Stage Three focus on?

Our methodology concerning how we taught was straight-forward: Hear, See, Do. In Stage One, the trainees *hear* the Word of God concerning healing and wholeness. In Stage Two, they begin to experience the outworking of prayer ministry and *see* the results in their own lives and in the lives of those for whom they pray.

2 Timothy 2:2 had always been deep in my spirit as a core scripture for Pierrepont. "And the things you have heard me say in the presence of many witnesses entrust to reliable men who will also be qualified to teach others."

As I considered the idea of a Stage Three, I became convinced that this verse was to be the key verse for the curriculum. We needed a stage for trainees to learn to teach all they had gained in Stages 1 and 2. We needed a "Do" stage for those trainees ready to be entrusted to teach others.

Realising the team was only now getting the curriculum for Stages One and Two under their belts, it was with not a little trepidation that I shared what I believed the Holy Spirit was saying. We needed a Stage Three!

## WHO WOULD COME?

The idea was for selected trainees (those with the 2 Timothy 2:2 reliability) to have a stage where they consolidated what they had learned, and took what they had learned to a deeper level. There had been so much teaching in Stages One and Two, and Stage Three would give them a chance to go deeper into the topics that impacted their lives and personal ministry.

Stage Three would be a stage for trainees who wanted to learn how to *teach* what they had learned of healing and deliverance. The trainees would be given an opportunity to practise teaching in front of their peers and the Pierrepont team. Where appropriate, some could also be invited to teach under supervision on Ellel Ministries' events.

Above all, Stage Three trainees would head out to teach and minister on a mission trip. This mission trip would be to a country where they could go deeper into issues not often found in the UK. They would have an opportunity to see poverty as many of them had never seen before, and yet come back to the UK and have their eyes opened to the lack of spirituality *in this country* in a way they had never seen before. I wanted to envision the Stage Three trainees with Ellel's vision of bringing hope and healing to a hurting world.

We decided that a Stage Three trainee would need to have had a certain amount of healing in their own lives. They needed to be ready to minister at a deeper level than they had previously experienced in perhaps their home churches or even on Stages One and Two. They also needed to have appropriate language skills, as they would be teaching in English.

You need to have a certain strength to do Stage Three... and above all, a Stage Three trainee wants to do more for the Lord. *They want more.*

## THE FIRST STAGE THREE

Our classroom was the skylight lounge, just across from the Great Hall. We had no course notes and no team member recording the teaching. We were pioneering – again!

Eighteen-year-old American Kimberly Bounds became our recording person. She recorded the teaching as well as being one of the trainees. No matter how old or young they were,[2] everyone on the course chipped in with that pioneering spirit that made it all work.

Most people who became Stage Three trainees had recently finished NETS 5, though only just. Most of them completed Stages One and Two, then had a few days holiday before digging into a brand-new stage. This was quite a challenge for both trainees and teachers.

Judy Miller[3] was part of that very first Stage Three. She had taken the Glyndley Manor Nine Week School and was seeking the Lord for her next adventure with Him. Just a few days before Stage Three started, Judy was at home in Colchester when a brown envelope came through the door. We had sent out a flyer letting people who had attended certain courses know about this opportunity – to learn to teach and go deeper into prayer ministry.

She says: "I was excited to read about this new thing offered at Ellel called Stage Three, and as I read the leaflet explaining the course, an arrow went straight into my spirit and I said, 'Yes, this is for me!' I rang up to find out if I could go on it. With the training I already had under my belt, the answer was 'yes'." "God's timing was perfect," Judy recalls. "I enquired at the beginning of the week, and by the Sunday I was at Ellel Pierrepont starting the course. Only then did I realise that *a mission trip* was part of the course. I knew in my spirit that this Stage Three was for me. Do you know how you say 'Yes!' to the Lord when you might not know all the details, but you just know you want more of Him and are ready to go wherever He sends you? Well, I certainly wanted more!"

There were thirteen trainees like Judy with quite a pioneering spirit on that first Stage Three.

## PUTTING TEACHING INTO PRACTICE

In preparation, I spent time with the Lord, getting His direction for this new curriculum.

"Jill," I heard the Father say, "they need to know My Word in their knower!"

"Their knower?" I questioned, but I knew *exactly* what my Father meant. These trainees needed to advance in the knowledge of their Lord and Saviour. They needed to *know* that they knew His love and His Word deep inside them. They needed to 'own it', as some say. What they had learned, perhaps as head knowledge, needed to travel deep down into their hearts. The gap between the mind and the heart is a real journey.

In the teaching sessions, I asked these trainees to look back over all they had learned in Stages One and Two. My aim was for each trainee to think clearly about how they would share or teach about the healing or deliverance *they had received* from the Lord; what they had learned concerning the topics they had previously studied. Often it is when you teach that you fully grasp what you have learned. As you teach it, you finally 'get it'.

Also, when people come to Pierrepont for a conference on a topic such as Freedom from Fear or the Christian Response to

Freemasonry, many of our visitors choose to receive some prayer ministry at the end of the day's teaching. I wanted Stage Three trainees to become confident in praying for others at events such as these, on a variety of topics.

At Ellel Ministries, we believe strongly that God's Word is the guide for our prayers. When we pray His principles, which are keys to the Kingdom of God, we see His hand on every situation. The trainees need to gain experience in both the teaching and ministry aspects of making disciples.

So prayer ministry is a vital part of the Stage Three curriculum. We gave the trainees some basic prayers to get started with, drawn from the course notes of Stages One and Two. These were not prayers to be memorised, but simply to be used as a guide, to help them remember the points for prayer when praying with people in need. Stage Three is all about equipping the trainees to handle as many situations as possible, while at the same time helping them understand that God wants to continue ministering to their own lives.

## WHERE WOULD WE GO?

As it happened, the Lord opened the door for our very first Stage Three mission trip in an unusual manner. The Reverend Doctor Cecilia Campbell visited Pierrepont to attend several courses while she was living in London. A Christian, Cecilia was originally from Ghana, and was doing her legal training at Middle Temple, one of the world's foremost centres of legal education and practice. During her visits to Pierrepont, we became great friends.

Something we see happening again and again with Christians who spend time in this country and get to know Ellel Ministries is this: they want to take the teaching back home. Cecilia wanted more of Ellel's teaching for the people in her own country. She had many, many influential connections, because her father was the private secretary of the King of the Ashanti tribe. She seemed to know just about everyone in Ghana, especially as she had about fifty brothers or sisters, many with church as well as royal connections.

So Cecilia invited us to come to Ghana for our first Stage Three mission trip. We agreed it would be a very good first mission location.

## THE FIRST MISSION TRIP

When we arrived, Accra airport was packed. And I mean the type of 'packed' where you can hardly move. We could hardly walk to find our baggage and make it out to the coach. People were offering to take our luggage – which we might never see again.

Some of the trainees felt a little insecure as they prepared for that first mission trip. Some were not widely travelled, while others, although they were experienced travellers, had never been to a country such as Ghana. However, for many, when they stepped off the plane, it was love at first sight.

"It was a different world," explained Judy. "One where I had never, ever ventured, and I knew this was the start of God's new adventure for me. I love Africa; I always will. You are totally out of your depth many times, and in God's hands. The heat, the smells, the food, the love and laughter, the serious challenges, the poverty, the history, the riches; it is all amazing."

What some loved, others definitely found a challenge. This gave me an even greater understanding of 2 Timothy 2:2. We would need to help the trainees resolve all sorts of feelings, emotions and confidence levels as they proved to themselves that they were reliable and up to the challenge of mission. While they may have seemed confident back in the UK, those that needed to be 'in control', in whatever way and for whatever reason, would find a mission trip difficult. As well as teaching, praying, healing and handling deliverance at a level deeper than experienced in the UK, some now faced the challenge of flexibility at a whole new level.

## FLEXIBLE

When we finally got to our first hotel in Accra, we found that there were some challenges. In one of the rooms, when we flushed the toilet, the whole cistern fell off the wall. In another room there was no running water, and in another room a blocked drain overflowed with water. But the final straw came when somebody had a shower and got an electric shock when they touched the cubicle. Thankfully, we were able to move quickly into a brand-new hotel. We were doubly blessed for our trouble, as this hotel had a very nice swimming pool.

I and my leadership team learned that even in Stage Three we – and the trainees – could possibly need prayer ministry. Things come up within you as you adapt to new and very different environments. This was great training for expecting the unexpected, and learning just how patient we all were (or were not) with other cultures, as well as working with others on the team; not to mention learning about our own patience and levels of flexibility.

## NATHANIEL

Nathaniel, soon called Nat by everyone, was our translator. He was a member of the large Calvary Baptist Church in Accra and spoke English to a very high standard. We got on very well, and he eventually came to Pierrepont as a NETS trainee himself. Nat worked hard to make us welcome, and assisted us every step of the way as we began our teaching in Ghana.

One of the skills many Stage Three trainees learn is how to teach while working with a translator. It is a skill in itself. You have to learn how to pace every word you say, and sometimes you need to assist the translator in presenting concepts which have a cultural context. You need to be aware of hand gestures that may or may not be acceptable in another country. Once again, you need to have a certain flexibility in working with someone from a totally different background, as they enable you to present the teaching to their homeland.

Working with a translator is a key skill developed on most of these mission trips even now, years later. It is a feature of nearly every mission trip. Learning how to teach effectively enables us to bring alive the Word of God. Paul says that "Through him and for his name's sake, we received grace and apostleship *to call people* from among all the Gentiles to the obedience that comes from faith" (Romans 1:5, my italics). We serve God with our whole heart, and that involves more than sharing a curriculum; it is also about the way we work together and encourage each other's faith.[4]

## FLEXIBLE PRAYER MINISTRY

On one of those first sessions in Ghana, I was teaching on physical healing. At the end of my talk, I called up people who had physical healing needs. There was hardly anybody left in their seat. A massive number of people came up to the front. I motioned for our Stage Three trainees to come up to pray for the people. They now had to step up to a new level as a prayer ministry team. There was no time to read a notebook of prayers, they had to rely on what the Holy Spirit was saying to them, and they had to know the Word of God. I prayed the Holy Spirit would bring to mind whatever they needed to remember. I prayed for everyone from the front first, and in that time I gave certain instructions to the crowd as to what the trainees would do, and now the trainees needed to have faith for a breakthrough in their confidence.

"I was absolutely amazed," Judy Miller recalls, "how Jill handled this. She was not at all flabbergasted at the numbers of people and the range of ailments. She divided the people into groups according to their particular ailment and then we as a team would take one of the groups."

"But when we hadn't prayed with such large numbers before, it was a major step for us; to be faced with a group of people telling you their ailments and they speak it out with an expectation that God is going to meet with them. Here we were in a totally different culture and with a new level of responsibility. Even though I was quite anxious inside, as all these people came up for prayer, there was a breakthrough for me into a new level of confidence in what God was calling me to do at that moment. You begin to cry out to God at a deeper level than ever before, crying out for God to meet with you and to enable you to pray with His authority. It is a step of growth."

A significant number of people were healed at that conference and we all grew in faith.

## QUALIFIED?

There is a great temptation, when you are on an overseas mission trip, to wonder in the middle of it all, "Just what makes you think you can do this?" When we are stepping up to a new level of obedience that comes from faith, we can long to fall back on the world's qualifications for accomplishing a task. But God has His own set of qualifications when it comes to serving Him.

We were reminded of this by one of Ghana's prominent bishops who graciously agreed to meet with us. Speaking of being qualified for the task, the bishop said, "I know P-H-D. Prayer. Healing. Deliverance."

The Lord was reminding us that it was *His* anointing that would be our accreditation. While we must be diligent to be approved in the Word (2 Timothy 2:15), it is not pieces of paper that enable our wobbly feet to stand on solid ground; it is the anointing of the Holy Spirit. It was the same message that the Lord had given me before I started working for Him at Pierrepont. We left our meeting with the bishop encouraged, and with a renewed focus on our mission to teach the keys of the Kingdom concerning Prayer, Healing and Deliverance.

## ONWARD AND UPWARD

Cecilia Campbell and I had an idea that someday we would love to see an Ellel centre in Ghana. We had no idea if this would ever be accomplished, but one thing we knew for certain was that before anything like that could happen, we would need the King of kings to command it – and the King of the Ashantis in Ghana to be in agreement.

So, Cecilia arranged for me and our very first Stage Three mission trip to meet the King of the Ashantis.

Most of us had never been to Africa before and here we were, heading straight to visit a king – the chief of a major tribe. Many of the trainees hadn't even thought in terms of tribes before. It was quite a stretch to imagine how this visit would go.

"We travelled to a big field," Martin Knapp remembers, "and we saw all these people in one place. The king was holding court under a huge palm tree and his elders were surrounding him in a horseshoe shape. They were all in tribal dress. One man was waving a large palm to keep the king relatively cool. And a group of albino women were standing behind the king; I think we felt as if we were missionaries from a century ago. It was most amazing."

I had to bring up the Stage Three mission group in front of the tribal elders, and as they passed by the elders, who were all scrutinising them, they had to stand in formation and not look at the king. I noticed the elders all had grim faces. I think they were sizing us up!

I was allowed to speak for a few minutes; again, not facing the king and once again speaking through a translator. I had to turn to the left, towards the translator and speak my carefully considered words. I believe the king thoroughly understood English, but it was about honour and respect for a king, and for those around to hear and understand what was being said. What was being said by me had to do with asking for a piece of land.

Cecilia and I wanted the king to grant permission for us to have a piece of land to use as an Ellel centre, which he did. He was most gracious in providing it, though even to this day we await the Lord's timing for the Ellel centre.

At the end of this visit, the Stage Three trainees all walked formally past the elders again and gave a little bow. With God, life is an adventure!

Back home the trainees put together a newsletter about all they had done and all they had learned, telling others about Stage Three.

## THE SECOND STAGE THREE

"As a trainee on the second Stage Three," recalls Morna Gillespie, "we were aware that those who had been on the first mission trip had rooted out the things that didn't work, and improved the things that did work."

We now had teaching notes, and Martin and Ginny Knapp,[5] who were very experienced people, were teaching the trainees. Clive Carr[6] came for a week and took Stage Three out on the streets to practise evangelism. In addition to teaching, Clive had a gift for showing trainees how to take every moment and turn it into an evangelistic opportunity.

Teaching is often a major hurdle for a lot of people, so we taught them how to improve their teaching skills for new and different environments.

While many people come on Stage Three because they want to learn how to teach, there is one thing that remains constant on mission – the element of uncertainty! When on overseas mission, you are always dealing with not being in control. Here at Pierrepont, when doing teaching practise we often draw the names out of a hat, and say, "… and all right, you are on!" You may not have much notice as to when or where you may be called to teach on a mission trip, so we keep the idea of always being prepared as a core element of Stage Three teaching.

## NEW LOCATIONS FOR MISSION TRIPS

When planning the Stage Three mission trip, we try to go to a particular country two or three times. The first year is the real pioneering year. This is where we are often carrying out groundbreaking initiatives, getting to know people in a new country and bringing teaching.

The next year we try to go to the same place. With established contacts, we have the opportunity to improve and deepen relationships. We can then enable local communities to take the teaching to new groups of people – people who are often better reached through the local people we came to know and love in our first trip. Occasionally we will do a third year to that country, but we will try to change the locations within that country. In certain ways, we are always pioneering, and you need to have a pioneering spirit. That is the essence of Stage Three.

Morna Gillespie, who went on to become deputy director of Pierrepont and has assisted with many, many Stage Three trips, recalls: "On one mission trip, pastors who didn't know us or anything about Ellel Ministries, came in suits and initially listened with some reserve to what we had to say. By the end they were wearing their African clothes and we were being called 'Sister Morna' and so on. It took a couple of days to get to know us, but when they did we were considered 'family'. The church visits at the end of that conference were amazing. We could have gone to any church – thirty or so – invited by those pastors. It was good to be training the pastors who were going to take the teaching to their churches."

## WHEN IT GOES WRONG

In 2008 we had to cancel a mission trip to India because of bombings in Mumbai. We only had ten days to re-prepare our hearts, our focus and the mission details, before we were to board the plane not for India but to Malaysia, to the Cameron Highlands.

It is never easy to change a mission location at the last minute – all the preparation you do, the cultural as well as spiritual. It calls for a deep faith that the Lord knows what He is doing. In ten days we had to have a complete turnaround of expectations. This was one of our greatest challenges, and I consider it one of God's gracious miracles that hearts and minds became forgiving and flexible enough to go forward to a new destination for that mission trip at such short notice.

## WHEN IT *REALLY* GOES WRONG

We tried again to head to India for our next mission trip. As usual, the trainees and staff who needed visas had sent their passports to the embassy in London. The day before we were due to fly out, the Stage Three trainees' passports arrived back at Pierrepont. It was a great shock to find we had not received the visas. No visa, no mission trip. There was nothing we, the leadership at Pierrepont, could do. There was trouble again in India and the British consulate said it was too dangerous to travel.

We spent the first days after receiving this terrible news dealing with loss, discouragement and anger. What was God saying in all of this? Was there a reason why He hadn't come through? These first days were an exercise in regrouping.

"What do we learn out of this?" we asked ourselves and we asked each other as we prayed. We longed to know what God had in mind.

There were one or two trainees who had been fearful of going to India, so they had to work through guilt feelings, as if they were responsible. Some were angry with Pierrepont. We had to say, "I'm sorry, you have just lost all this money", because it had been necessary to book non-refundable flights *before* getting the visas.[7] We had lost £7,000 in non-refundable flights.

Thankfully, by the grace of God, someone donated that entire amount so we could refund the trainees. Everything was refunded! That was no small miracle to us. All the expectations, all the work and preparation, all hope of an overseas mission trip had gone out of the window.

Then one of the trainees helped to bring something good out of an unbelievably distressing situation. Sui Man, who was from Hong Kong, contacted her Chinese church in Leicester. We could go to that church the very next week and bring a team to teach, and lead prayer ministry.

We taught in English and it was translated into Cantonese. This kept the translation experience, and meant everyone was working in a very different culture. It was not what the trainees expected when they signed up and paid for Stage Three, but it turned out to be an amazing experience.

The turnaround in our hearts and minds took a few days, not to mention the fact that we had to make arrangements with the church and sort out accommodation. We had to adapt the timetable to accommodate when the Chinese people of that community could attend, but it was brilliant, it was excellent.

Two of the Chinese people from Leicester came on NETS and this blessing of a suddenly rearranged mission trip continued to bless even more trainees when we later held 'Chinese NETS'. This was a very new way of teaching NETS (Stages One and Two), totally translated into Mandarin, and it meant we had trainees from all over East Asia, some of whom only spoke Mandarin. They were able to visit the Mandarin-speaking congregation of this wonderful church in Leicester and practise teaching and ministering in their own language, before heading home.

## ULRIKE'S STORY

Although Stage Three focuses on developing ministry and teaching skills, God continues to heal the trainees. It takes time for the teaching you have already heard to trickle down from your head to your heart. As we use what we have learned, we are processing it and applying it. Ulrike's story is a good example of this. Ulrike is from Germany and she joined us for Stage Three in 2007:

> I was on Stages One and Two of NETS 5 in 1999 to 2000. In those months I experienced so much healing and deliverance that it really made a new person out of me. Or better to say that eventually I was finally free to be me!
>
> Then in spring 2007, I came back to do Stage Three of NETS. On one of the weekends there was a course about sex and sexuality and the Stage Three trainees were asked to help with the prayer ministry. At first I wasn't even sure if I could do this because I had a terrible headache, but after the Ministry Office leader prayed for me, it was gone. Before we started we were told that many people come for prayer ministry on that course and therefore we should try not to spend too much time with one person.
>
> Ministry time began and our first guest shared with us that since childhood, her eyes were always drawn to unclean pictures. While I listened, the Holy Spirit put something in my mind: I had the same problem. Whenever there was an unclean picture, my eyes were drawn to it and I could hardly get it out of my mind again. I do not have a TV and I definitely don't buy those kind of magazines, but pictures like that are found in many places (at least in Germany), places like advertisements in the streets or on the counter of a gas station where it is almost impossible to avoid seeing them. I had received prayer into this area twice, but it hadn't changed.
>
> I remembered something that happened to me when I was about eleven. A neighbour on our camping site came into

137

our caravan when my friend and I were there without my parents for a couple of hours. He showed us a pornography magazine – page by page. I was shocked; full of fear and shame but at the same time also curious. After a while he left. I didn't tell this to my parents because of the shame and guilt I felt.

I knew that this was an important key for getting free – something for me to bring to a personal ministry appointment soon! However, at the time I kept on listening to and praying for our guest. The Lord blessed the guest and then a second person came, but after that, to our surprise no one else came for prayer.

The lead counsellor and I were talking quietly while I sensed more and more intensely that NOW was the time to get rid of that old stuff. I tried to convince the Holy Spirit that this wasn't a good moment, but He didn't seem to change His mind! So carefully I shared the whole thing with the lead counsellor, assuring her that it would need only a quick prayer, and that we could stop immediately if someone came to us for ministry. Praise God, she was willing to pray for me.

While she was doing so, I was reminded of a disgusting figure that my father brought home one day when I was maybe ten. I told her this and again she prayed for me. Then I couldn't believe it, but there was a third incident that I was reminded of next. It was my father bringing something home that he bought in a sex shop when I was fifteen. A quick prayer into this and – can you believe it? – a fourth situation came to my mind. This time it was a stranger who touched me once in an inappropriate way when I was nine or so.

While the counsellor was also praying into this, amazingly no more guests came, either to us or to the other prayer teams. I was so embarrassed. Not because of the things that happened in the past, but because I was receiving ministry at a time when I should have been the one to minister to others! But God's grace is overwhelming. This whole situation did not last longer than ten to fifteen minutes but it brought change for a lifetime.

One year later, a friend and I went to see a funny movie that was suitable for children of six and older. We went to the movie theatre, only to leave it again after twenty minutes because what we found was one scene after the other with a very clear sexual meaning. I was angry – not only because of the waste of money but also because I knew that I had those pictures in my mind again.

The next morning as I was waking up, I realised that none of the pictures were there. Instead I saw a picture from the Holy Spirit: a piece of wood with four hooks screwed into it. Then I saw the same wood but without the hooks. And I understood that those four situations we had prayed about on NETS were like hooks in my soul. Whenever I saw something unclean – even when it was unintentional – it got stuck on one of those hooks and my eyes were drawn to it. BUT NOW THE HOOKS WERE NOT THERE ANYMORE! My, was I happy to realise this! A great joy over the power of the blood of Jesus filled my heart. Finally I was free! This sense of being drawn to those pictures is gone also. For instance, now when I drive by an advertisement showing almost naked women it doesn't affect me anymore. What a relief! Isn't He amazing?

A few months later I had the chance to share this for the first time during a teaching time. I got myself a flat piece of wood and screwed hooks into it. I made loops [in] some shoelaces. They symbolised the pictures. Without the hooks, the shoelaces could not stay on the wood. My goal was to make clear how important it is to get to the root of the problem instead of praying into the symptoms only!

During NETS 5 I had learned to ask what I call the million dollar question: "What is the root of this problem and when did it came into your/my life?" The answer to this question

shown by the Holy Spirit is the beginning of being healed and/
or getting free. And that is worth a million dollars!

I could write a book about how NETS has affected my life.
Maybe when I retire!

*Chapter Thirteen*

# You Are My Rock

*… You have given the commandment to save me, for You are my
rock and my fortress*

(Psalm 71:3 NKJV)

I sat on the edge of my seat at the doctor's office, next to my
husband. We could hardly believe the diagnosis – that Ron had lung
cancer. A few days later, Ron would stand up before the little church
we helped to start in Frensham and share the news that he had only
six months to live.

Ron's personal and financial papers were in order, and he had
built so much in our house (cabinets and practical items) which
enabled us to live comfortably. He had given sacrificially to the
ministry in ways that are still bearing fruit. He was a man of godly
order in every area of his life. He was a quiet man, but when he
spoke, everyone listened.

The weeks passed quickly and the six-month timescale proved
to be fairly accurate.

As I sat at the edge of his bed during the last days of Ron's life,
he spoke about Pierrepont. His only concern was that I should
know deep inside of me that I had his blessing for carrying on the

work of this ministry. He released me into the work we had started together, saying that nothing was to hold me back.

In those quiet moments a peace came and covered us with a blessing. We prayed together, telling the Lord that we were holding each other lightly on the palms of our hands. As he released me into the work of Pierrepont, together we released the future of Pierrepont back to our Father who had started this work, whose work it was and is. These last times of sharing together were some of our deepest and holiest moments.

On the day he died, I had left him early in the morning with Inus Joubert. Inus' wife, Julia, had been my PA for six years and they had met and married at Pierrepont. In the last month of Ron's terminal illness, they had both moved into our home to help. Ron wanted to die at home, not in a hospice, and without them I could not have done it. On that last Saturday I was teaching at a conference in Ealing, London, which was jointly run by Ellel Ministries and Premier Radio. When I was on my lunch break, Inus phoned to say I needed to come back straight away. Another member of the team took over the teaching and I went home immediately.

When I arrived, Ron was semi-conscious. We sang one of our favourite worship songs together and then we sat Ron up. His eyes opened briefly and I said, "Ron, I release you to go to Jesus. You don't need to stay here for me." In that moment he took his last breath and went home. God dropped a scripture into my heart from Psalm 116:15 – "Precious in the sight of the LORD is the death of his saints." And then I released Ron to the Lord.

If you have ever experienced the death of a loved one who is a believer, if you were able to stay at their side as Jesus came to take them home, perhaps, like me, you will have felt the truth of the verse, "Oh death, where is thy sting?" (1 Corinthians 15:55, KJV). For me it was not a moment of tears, but it was a time of peace beyond my human understanding. I had also received a blessing from Ron that released me more deeply than ever before into the work set before me at Ellel Pierrepont. I believe that when the Father calls us to hold the things we love lightly in the open palm of our hand, not squeezing tight and refusing to let go, He gives back to us in full measure.

## STAGE FOUR

It was about the time of Ron's death that I and the Pierrepont leadership team felt we were released by God to develop the fourth stage of NETS, completing the original vision for a one-year programme.

As we sought the Lord, it seemed that Stage Four was to be a time for enabling trainees to develop their own personal ministry. This would be the stage that would pull together the first three stages and answer the question, "OK, what am I going to do with what I have learned?"

Stage Four would also be a time of special personal mentoring of trainees. The purpose was for them to be equipped and released into the ministry of their own calling.

## AN ACADEMIC PHASE

When we started the first Stage Four in 2007, we went through a short phase of having quite an academic format. Trainees were required to write a paper or several essays. While Stage Three called for practical teaching, this new stage's more academic approach suited some, but not all.

To support the academic side we developed our library at that time, and received an amazing blessing when Christ For The Nations closed their Bible college in Bognor Regis, Sussex and gave us their entire library. They donated over 6,000 books, including the complete set of Spurgeon's sermons and the Müller diaries – classic works – along with other good books by this generation and many missionary biographies. We are so grateful for this wonderful resource, which is well used.

The academic phase did not last long, however, as it became clear that the Lord's plan for NETS was that we should continue with the more practical "hear, see, do" style of training which we had had from the start. Though sound academic study is often a good basis for ministry, and we strongly encourage Bible study, Stage Four does not now focus on the academic. It has been fine-tuned into a much more practical tool to help trainees develop their own gifting and ministry. Essays are no longer required. Each trainee has a personal mentor to help them discover and refine their own gifting. Alongside gifting, we look at character. Many a well-intentioned and gifted leader has fallen due to lack of godly character, so developing character is essential.

# CHARACTER

As part of Stage Four, trainees write out a timeline of their life, looking at the good things God has done and the gifts that are evident in their lives. They acknowledge the pain of the past, and the healing that has happened and is still ongoing. Often the Lord calls us to establish a ministry from out of our 'mess', but for us to be strong enough to carry out that ministry long-term we must also have a well-developed and godly character.

In Ezekiel 3:14 the prophet recognised that at the beginning of his ministry, "the hand of the LORD was strong upon me" (NKJV). This is a time for trainees to discover where the hand of the Lord is most strong upon *them*. When God has touched your life, you will want to reach out to others (Luke 22:32b) and often it is in the places where God has touched us that we have most to give to others.

Our aim in Stage Four is to release men and women into their own God-given destiny and ministry, but often you wonder if you can get there from here! As well as needing to know what God is calling them to, and where, each trainee also needs to discover the very practical 'how'. Some people have an unrealistic understanding of what God might be calling them to do, and so we assist each trainee as honestly as possible to appraise the direction God is taking them in, encouraging them all along the way.

So Stage Four was firmly established, and I am thrilled that we now have a complete year of training available for those who wish to complete the full NETS course.

## A NEW HUSBAND

It was about this time that I met a man called Colin Jones. As we got to know each other, we began to see that God was bringing us together for a purpose. Colin is a Christian, with a heart for the Lord's work, and he had undertaken the Nine Week School at Ellel Canada in 1999. He was eager to see people trained and equipped to set others free in Christ.

We eventually married, three years after Ron's death, and I was very pleased to discover that Colin and I made good travel partners. While Ron had stayed at home, quietly supporting the work, Colin is more directly involved. He is a member of the Pierrepont ministry team and accompanies me on many teaching trips. As we are entering our golden years, Colin and I make a good team; both of us want to see Christians equipped and trained for the call of God on their lives – whether that is through coming to Pierrepont for NETS, going to another Ellel centre, or wherever the Lord leads them. I do thank God for giving me Colin – he is a wonderful support to me and to many others.

## PAPUA NEW GUINEA

Earlier in this book I mentioned that when I was a small girl of seven, a neighbour had asked my mother if she could take me to her chapel where a missionary was showing slides of his work.

At the end he gave an appeal for anyone who felt God may be calling them to go as a missionary to Papua New Guinea to come forward. I immediately went to the front and I was the only one! He prayed that if this calling I felt was God speaking, that one day God would indeed take me to Papua New Guinea to preach His gospel.

As the wheels of the plane touched down in Papua New Guinea, I recalled the memory of that day – standing at the front of the church and telling my mother when I got home that "one day I will go to Papua New Guinea and preach the gospel". With a lump in my throat I felt every motion of the wheels touching the tarmac.

A NETS trainee, Julian Kivori from Papua New Guinea, had asked me if I would be willing to go to his country and share the Ellel teaching about healing and deliverance. He must have been quite surprised when I so readily said, "Yes!"

As the door of the plane opened, the smells and fresh hot air hit our faces as we set out to share the teaching the Lord had given us. And now, in this land, God has established a new Ellel centre. Who would have believed all those years ago that there would be an Ellel PNG?

"The gifts and calling of God are irrevocable,"[1] I said to myself as I exited that plane, but it is so much easier *now* to see the hand of the Father than it was on that day when I stood all alone in front of a church, so young.

Today, blessed with a godly husband, a godly companion for the travel that is required for this work and for this stage of our life's journey, we are also looking for ways to hand on the baton to those whom God is calling. I share this story of the Miracles of Pierrepont to inspire others with the truth that God is looking for people who will stand in the gap between what you see happening in your country and the way we are all called to live; those who will give Him the glory.

## GOING GLOBAL

Back in 1993 Joe and Ruth Hawkey were the directors of Glyndley Manor, where I did the Nine Week School. When I was commissioned, Joe prophesied over me that I would teach in every continent of the world. It is stunningly amazing to look back now, more than twenty years later, to see that I have indeed taught in every continent of the world, except Antarctica. Many people from the nations I taught in subsequently took time out to come on NETS.

To date we have had 1,347 trainees attending NETS from 74 different countries. Incredible!

The Lord has taken me to Australia, New Zealand, Singapore, Taiwan, Hong Kong, Malaysia, Thailand, Japan, Papua New Guinea, Colombia, Canada, USA, Ghana, Kenya, South Africa, Hungary, Russia, Ukraine, Poland, Romania, Norway, Sweden, France, Germany, Switzerland, The Netherlands and other countries. The Lord has always cared for me and provided in many amazing ways.

As God is our Father, there is always *one more story*, one more miracle to share. I want to finish this book with yet another miracle that I believe shows just how He cares for us in the details of our lives. It's a story of what happened to my passport…

## SWEDEN: THE PASSPORT STORY

From Pierrepont we had been supporting the Ellel Ministries work in Sweden, and a team would go out once a month to teach a weekend course. Ryanair started doing trips from London Luton to an out-of-city airport near Stockholm for £1 per person, each way, which enabled us to take quite a large team of people who could pray and support the teaching.

On one of these occasions at Luton Airport, I had my boarding pass and passport in my hand in the departure lounge when

I received a mobile call of a private nature, so I went over to the window to take myself out of earshot. The window consisted of two panes of thick glass stretching the length of the building with a small gap in between. I could never understand how I did this, but somehow I dropped my passport down the gap in between the two panes of glass. The flight was now being called, and you could see my passport about twelve feet down – but obviously I couldn't get to it!

I alerted the desk staff to my predicament and many of the passengers came over to have a look. The ground staff told me with no uncertainty that I could not board the plane without my passport and people were now boarding. We started to pray. It seemed utterly hopeless – people came over and made various suggestions, but the ground staff said I would need to wait behind from the flight in the hope that a maintenance man could come and maybe somehow reach the passport.

Even then they weren't hopeful. Julia (my PA) and I really started to pray. "Oh Lord," I said, "I really need to be on this flight with my passport. Can You make it happen somehow?" And somehow I knew God would send an angel.

A lady came over with a large reel of the sticky tape that goes around your case when you are checking it in – the kind that adheres to itself. She lowered the sticky tape down the twelve or so feet until it reached my passport. We saw the sticky tape touch the passport but fall off again. She tried once more and this time the tape stuck to the spine side of the passport and she gently pulled it up and handed it to me.

My heart was racing as I gave thanks to God – but the woman disappeared before I could thank her. I ran to the boarding gate and said, "Would you thank the lady with the white blouse who helped me get my passport?" and they said, "There isn't a lady with a white blouse that works here – all our staff have got the regulation navy blue uniform." So I said, "She was here a second ago and she got my passport for me!" and they said, "We don't know any such lady."

"Can I get on to the flight?"

We were told to run out to the plane and see if they could still let us on. Julia and I tore outside and found the plane with everybody on board and the steps starting to move away. Thankfully when they saw us, they started to put the steps back in place for us. As we boarded the flight everybody clapped, and as we took our seats, Ione Carver said to me, "You did realise that was an angel, didn't you?"

As we sat in our places and fastened our seatbelts, both Julia and I did indeed realise that actually God had sent an angel to get my passport back for me. Later in Sweden, as I told the story, people were deeply impacted. We simply do not fully understand or recognise the way in which angels are sent by God to assist us in our times of need.

Do we not serve an amazing God? Yes, we do. This is His work. This is His story, and by His grace He allows us to have a part. Who would settle for a boring life, when you can have such an adventure with Him? He is good *all the time*.

## THE TRUE MIRACLE

We have learned that the true miracle of Pierrepont has been more than the supply of every knife, fork and spoon, or beds for trainees or answered prayers for the daily provision of a ministry which was God's idea and is His work. That is only a small part of what He wants to supply as He changes stony hearts into hearts of flesh,[2] teaches us the love of the Good Shepherd and continues to lead all of us, His under-shepherds, His servants in all nations. We have learned again and again that we can trust Him at all times with our personal needs, as we put our hands to the plough of His work.

But the true miracle of Pierrepont, and of every Ellel centre, is the miracle of God's healing and deliverance in so many lives. This is a truly extraordinary gift from the loving heavenly Father. Even more, He is *our* Father. He will teach us how to be mothers and fathers to others; how to train the children and the flock in His nurture, His ways, His salvation. He has established our feet upon a rock that cannot be moved; not now and not in the future. As we go into the future, we must not be quiet.

> *I proclaim righteousness in the great assembly; I do not seal my lips, as you know, O Lord.....I speak of Your faithfulness and salvation.*
>
> (Psalm 40:9, 10)

> *I will say of the Lord, He is my refuge and my fortress, my God in whom I trust.*
>
> (Psalm 91: 2)

> *For great is the Lord and most worthy of praise.*
>
> (Psalm 96: 4a)

# Testimonies

I first came to Ellel Pierrepont in 2011 for a Jesus Heals Today conference. What a day that was – and what a wonderful first experience of God's presence in a way that I had not known before.

But the real turnaround for me took place in three significant events in 2012. First of all, MicroNETS in February where, for the first time ever, I sobbed my heart out to God and He was able to break through into my life in a way that I had been longing for – for a long, long time – but had never seemed to get to. God did an immense healing work in me that week – dealing with things which had shut Him out of certain areas of my life and helping me to become more rooted and grounded in His love.

Then it was at the Getting to the Root of Fear and Lies weekend in April that even more significant changes took place. For the first time ever, I really experienced what it was to be loved by God, to know Him as my tender Father and to rejoice in that love. I was important and I mattered to Him and that totally changed my perspective of myself and of Him. I will always treasure that weekend, because God did many amazing and incredible things.

Then, I was fortunate to come to another Jesus Heals Today session in May and was able to bring some friends from my church, which was a testimony in itself. God revealed to me that I was His "beautiful daughter of the King of kings", a truth that I have had to guard and am still guarding, as His truth works its way into the very depths of my heart.

God has been opening me up in so many ways to His love and faithfulness. I am still learning and I am so thankful for what God has done and also to all the faithful and prayerful people involved in Ellel. Thank you for expressing God's love and for being faithful and obedient, even when the sacrifice has cost much. May God bless you richly and continue to establish His work, for the glory of His Kingdom and to the lifting up of Jesus.

*Samantha*

~

The nine-day MicroNETS programme at Pierrepont was a turning point in my life. That week I finally realised and understood that Jesus wanted me to live a victorious life in Him. After MicroNETS I began to see Him setting me free from areas of bondage to sin, and healing me physically too. Prior to that I was struggling with an addiction to pornography and also a physical condition that caused random parts of my body to swell, and even threatened my life on one occasion when my throat swelled so much I had to be rushed to hospital. The biblical understanding I gained at Ellel Pierrepont was a huge key and has definitely changed my life. I have not found Christian training quite like this anywhere else.

*David*

~

I am twenty-seven years old now. I did NETS 26, Stages One and Two, and half a year later did stages Three and Four.

During my time on NETS Stages One and Two, God has brought an amazing healing to my life. Since I was sixteen years old I [have] suffered from emotional issues. I dropped out of school and received psychological care, and later psychiatric medication. I was using the medication permanently. When I was eighteen, I was hospitalised in a day care mental institution for two months. I eventually asked to be released, since it didn't do me any good.

The two types of medication I was on are very strong. In fact I found out that one of them is not permitted to be used anymore due to its dangers. During the first year on the medication, I gained more than thirty kg and became very fat, and that led me to more depression.

But our God is a healer! My healing journey began with a Christian counsellor who was very open to the gifts of the Holy Spirit, and during my time receiving counselling, I got off one of the medications, praise God! But I was still using the strongest medication of the two. On top of that, I was using medication to calm my nerves from time to time, and those were strong enough to put a horse to sleep (I am not a horse!). I was also using anti-acid medication for a severe stomach acid problem.

All that changed on NETS! God has set me free from all (ALL!!) dependence on medication, and I have been off psychiatric medication for more than a year now (after about ten years on them!). I no longer need the anti-acid medication, nor any other form of medication. On NETS, I not only met the healing power of God, but also His faithful workers, people that have dedicated their lives to serving God and to serving His children. To call it a life-changing experience would be an awful understatement. I became a believer when I was nineteen, but I was still dealing with lots of baggage from before. They say at Pierrepont that NETS stands for Never Ever The Same, and I have to fully agree; I also claim it stands for Non-Expiring True Salvation.

My mother ... told me after I did NETS, "I believe in Jesus, because I see what He has done in you."

*TP*

~

I came on NETS in October 2000. I had applied for a one-year sabbatical from my job, and one of the reasons I was given the time off was that I was in constant physical pain. The occupational health doctor was investigating whether I should be officially registered as disabled, as I had suffered for six years with severe joint pain in my wrists and elbows. The outworking of the pain was such that I couldn't even do simple everyday tasks such as tie my shoelaces or brush my teeth. Every morning when I woke up, my joints felt so hot I could have fried an egg on them!

In a communion service, about three weeks into NETS, the person leading the service, John Kilford, asked anyone who wanted prayer for physical healing to stand. I stood up fairly reluctantly – I had been prayed for many times over the years, and didn't really have much faith for my healing. However, I figured that if the Ellel Leadership had the faith, I would give it a try. What I didn't expect was that John then asked those sitting next to anyone who was standing to pray. I was standing surrounded by a bunch of NETS trainees. My attitude wasn't great – what did they know? They had only been there three weeks, just like me! Two lovely ladies from South Africa prayed for me. I honestly couldn't say I felt anything special, but I listened, thanked them and sat down.

When you have severe, constant pain you learn how to manage the pain. During that day I felt that I was managing the pain well, and during the next day, and the next... Finally I realised that there was no more pain, and that the heat in my joints wasn't there when I woke up in the morning. It took me two weeks to admit to myself that God had healed me.

It was several weeks later that Jesus revealed to me some of the keys for why I had had those six years of disability – among them were unforgiveness, breaking the Sabbath, pride and fear. I give Him all the glory and praise for healing me, and restoring me spirit, soul and body.

*Morna Gillespie*

~

The night before I came to Pierrepont on the first NETS course in 1997, I had wrestled with God and cried out to Him about my unknown future. I lay in bed with my right hand stretched out to Him, saying: "God, I choose to trust you for the future, even though this all feels rather terrifying." The next day I was shown my room at Pierrepont, and on my Welcome card was Isaiah 41:13: "For I am the LORD, your God, who takes hold of your right hand and says to you, Do not fear; I will help you."

Doing NETS transformed and informed me. A lot of what we were taught I had not heard before, and much of what I had previously heard had only been in theory. At Ellel I learned how to put the teaching into practice, resulting in life-changing impact and transformation!

One specific area of impact was the depth of God's love for me as a Father... yes, even me! I'd had no difficulty believing that God loved others with a passion, but was doubtful of His complete and utter acceptance of me. This affected my behaviour; I was always pushing boundaries to see if He would react and reject me. But over time, God revealed Himself to me in ways I could not have dreamed of. The legacy of this is a totally different perspective of life and living. Now I have a 'quiet confidence' (part of Isaiah 30:15) that allows me to live without anxiety over my future (or past!)

*Dee Arrand*

~

I did NETS Stage One and God provided everything I needed to do the course. Even though it did not look possible, God made provision. Since NETS, God is still showing me the same things. He just keeps on providing exactly what I need at the right time and I have come to realise that God can turn every impossible financial situation around and simply wants to show me that He is looking after me and is in control. I'm not striving now, working so many long hours like I used to. It's not so much the provision, but the way in which God provides that makes me feel happy! Bless you!

*Rebecca*

~

We were delighted when a ministry team from Ellel Pierrepont of over twenty people attended a healing day we hosted for our church in March 2012. The team were amazing. They came prepared for spiritual battle – united, prepared, organised and filled with the Spirit of God. It was an awesome day of healing, deliverance and hope for those who attended. The team operated in the gifts of the Spirit and demonstrated the love, compassion, humility and healing of Jesus Christ. Many reported the life-changing impact the day had on their lives.

We have been involved with Ellel Ministries for over ten years, attending workshops and courses at various ministry locations throughout the country. We have found the ministry to be outstanding, Spirit-filled and Spirit-led and have watched with great joy its expansion in the area of healing, restoration and deliverance.

We look forward to continue working with Ellel Ministries. They are very instrumental in God's end-time army, working to set captives free.

*Pastor Marva Bell (Wembley Family Church)*

~

The Lord began His healing work in me several years ago, and so when I went on NETS my primary thought was to be further equipped in ministry. But as I sat through the teachings and allowed myself to be ministered to, I began to realise that God was bringing me into His agenda, and not mine.

The twenty-weeks' training on healing, deliverance and discipleship was a milestone in my Christian walk. It was a remarkable time with the Lord, when He worked wonders in my life.

It is said that God can speak to us through the 'language' we understand. Well, I was an automotive electrician before the Lord called me into His ministry full-time. I remember rewiring a race car with a colleague. We totally stripped the car from all its old wiring system and ran new wires and fitted new electrical devices. During the twenty-weeks' NETS training, I felt like that race car in the hands of the Lord, being 'stripped down and rewired'.

Out of all God accomplished in me during those twenty weeks, three things stand out clearly:

1. God restored my true identity.
2. He was my heavenly DAD in whom I find true affirmation and acceptance.
3. He confirmed His calling in my life for a ministry of healing and discipleship for Papua New Guinea.

Since 2011, we have conducted many conferences and day courses in Papua New Guinea. They have all been successful, thanks to the Lord's blessing, and the impact continues to spread. Praise the Lord for Ellel Ministries' impact in such a time as this!

*Julian Kivori*

~

In January 1997 I walked up the drive of Pierrepont to join the very first NETS group. Evidently I was the first trainee to arrive. I did not know what to expect, but I certainly was not disappointed in all that God did in that six months. God had already given me a vision for the first Ellel centre in Australia but I was expecting that someone else would bring the vision to fruition. I left my four children and husband back in Australia, which was very painful, but with the pain came the healing. As the Lord healed me and set me free, He was truly preparing me for His call on my life. I discovered that my identity was in being a wife and mother and that God needed me to know my identity was in Him. NETS was the most rewarding six months of my life.

*Diane Watson*

# Epilogue

*No story of Pierrepont would be complete without a word of thanks to the Reverend Jim Graham, whose support and input has been invaluable. Jim Graham is Pastor Emeritus at Gold Hill Baptist Church (Chalfont, Buckinghamshire). Both he and his late wife, Anne, have been closely aligned with Ellel Ministries throughout the years.*

*He has mentored me personally with great wisdom and grace, prayerfully supporting me and the entire leadership team. He has also led leadership retreat days and prayed with us through the various challenges that have arisen over the years.*

*Jim is also an associate teacher and has taught on all of our NETS schools, on many other events at Pierrepont, at other Ellel centres, and at international conferences. Jim's teaching is hugely appreciated, especially because his humble, delightful character shines through everything. It is therefore fitting that Jim has written the epilogue to this book.*

Jill Southern-Jones

## CLOSING WORDS BY JIM GRAHAM

As I begin to write this last chapter of the Pierrepont story, I have just spent two weeks at Pierrepont. I was giving eight lectures to Stage Four (the final stage of NETS) on 'Discipling Others', as well as four sessions at one of the Pierrepont Understanding Days ('Understanding Prophecy'); giving three lectures to Stage Two of NETS on 'Real Discipleship'; taking two Bible studies ('Who is Jesus?' and 'What is the Church?') with MicroNETS and Stage Two trainees, and taking one session with MicroNETS on 'The Father Heart of God'.

I was unable to attend the communion service on the middle Friday morning of these two weeks – the central weekly event for the whole community at Pierrepont – where memory is powerfully stirred by the event of Calvary where God-made-flesh was crucified so that we might be cleansed, redeemed and made whole and where there is an intrusive personal and corporate encounter with the Lord Jesus in His risen, triumphant reality in the crowded conference hall.

In addition to all of this, teaching is given on Kingdom values and Kingdom living and healing through deliverance is explained, explored and experienced. Then there are the Healing Retreats, the personal ministry appointments, the church visits and the overseas mission trips. It all adds up to a pretty comprehensive programme of instruction and involvement.

As I looked out on these men and women from five continents, a bewildering number of different nations and from all walks of life, either in the Great Hall or in the conference centre, some receiving simultaneous translation in their native language – I did not only see them at their desks, but I saw thousands of lives being radically and forever transformed across the whole world as a result of their ministry and leadership. What a privilege! What a challenge! What a ministry! It's a far cry from the vision sketched on the back of an envelope and the stolen gates at the entrance to the drive. Many nights, at the close of the day, as I have driven back down the drive to tackle the M3 and the M25 motorways on my way home, I have been close to tears as I have reflected on the presence and the purposes of God experienced and unfolded during the course of the day.

You have read the story – the clear vision given to Peter Horrobin all these years ago of a 'teaching hospital' and his honest and inspiring leadership and presentation of that vision; the life-journey of Jill Southern-Jones so key, foundational, and crucial to it all; the picture of the globe rolling up the drive; the prophetic words, the biblical affirmations, the relentless, destiny-defining climate of heaven-rending prayer; the nagging uncertainties, the risk-taking, the willingness to explore new spiritual geography; the backbreaking physical exertion, the disappointments, the silence of heaven and the discovery that when God is silent He is not absent; the miraculous timing and appropriateness of God's provision; and far above and beyond everything else the unmistakable reality of the absolute faithfulness of God.

I am frequently asked about my relationship with Ellel Ministries as I travel around the United Kingdom. It always surprises me how ill-informed the Christian world chooses to be. Is there a spiritual battle going on here that contests the unveiling of this ministry to the Church in particular and the world in general? Is the cost of discipleship too high a price to pay? Is being made totally new in Christ by the power of the Holy Spirit too intrusive and awkward? You see, there are no secrets here. There is an excellent website. There is online teaching and daily devotionals. There are the books and the publishing company. The annual handbook and the available courses are publicised. There are the CDs and the DVDs. From time to time there are the international conferences held in the United Kingdom. What is there not to know?

I have been honoured to be associated with and involved in Ellel Ministries over the years. Long years ago I concluded that this ministry is about discipleship and discipling. My deeply considered perception is that the biggest question that faces the Church today is, 'How do we make disciples?' I have long since concluded that in the contemporary Western Church, we don't have a missional problem or a leadership problem or a 'How do we share the incredible news of Jesus with others?' problem. What we have is a discipleship problem.

When we begin to learn how to disciple people properly, we will always get mission and we will always produce leaders and we will make others realise the purpose for which they were created as we live the Jesus life in the power of the Holy Spirit before them. Clearly, Jesus never asked us to build His Church (that is the responsibility He came to fulfil!), but He has overtly called us to make disciples.

Part of the problem confronting the challenge to make disciples is that many of us, who become Christians through realising that fundamentally we are sinners, cut off from a living, vibrant relationship with God; repenting of our sin and recognising and responding to Jesus Christ as Lord and Saviour, bring lives that are wounded, broken and bound and we need healing, mending, and releasing. It takes time and patience, skill and humility, compassion and care to see that accomplished. It is so easy to hide in our theology rather than be exposed to reality.

So often the healers need to be healed first before they venture into a confused, bewildered, despairing, and fearful culture with confidence, hope and expectation. The Cross of Jesus certainly makes wholeness a possibility, but what is offered there needs to be apprehended. When our biblical theology is actually experienced as well as understood, we have a powerful security and stability to go to that culture, not simply to challenge it, but to change it – as its wounds are bound up, its hearts are healed, its imprisoned spirits released and its lives reclaimed and restored.

So the 'teaching hospital' that God put into Peter Horrobin's heart was born, in the leafy beauty of the south of England countryside. The instruction is rich in biblical content and theological integrity. However, more than faithful instruction is given there. It is a foundational conviction at Pierrepont that it is insufficient to say, "Listen to what I am telling you." Fundamental and important as propositional truth is, there is another strand that has to be displayed. Practical and personal imitation has to be demonstrated – "Let me show you how to do this." It might be more simply put in this form: I do, you watch; I do, you help;

You do, I help; You do, I watch. All of this in a safe and accepting environment without pretentiousness or arrogance. It was ever thus as we watch the Great Master Teacher and Healer Himself! The years have passed, lessons have been learned, adjustments have been made, mistakes have been corrected, but the heart and joy of Jesus has always been sought.

In a real sense, this is not the last chapter. It is the end of the beginning. Twenty crowded and eventful years have passed with all the successes and failures, laughter and tears, joys and sorrows, ecstasies and agonies, ups and downs, fulfilments and frustrations of divine ministry put into human hands. However, the fact remains that countless thousands have been released into freedom and service right around the world as a consequence of this 'teaching hospital' being brought into being. But the future beckons for as long as time and human history lasts. I was reminded of words written by the linguistic expert, Frank Laubach:

> When Christ was here on earth, He was limited to performing His ministry in one place and at one time. He was one man, walking beside one sea in one little corner of the earth. He healed whatever He touched, but His touch was necessarily limited by time and space.

> Now, does it make sense that the Father would send His Son for this limited ministry? I don't think that is tenable. He made provision to carry on the work through the Holy Spirit: we are to complete His mission. We are his multiplied hands, His feet, His voice, and compassionate heart. Imperfect and partial to be sure, but His healing Body just the same. It is through the Holy Spirit that we receive the power to carry on the work of the apostles. It is a challenging and sobering thought: when we receive the Holy Spirit into our lives, we receive the same urgent and life-giving force that led our Master.

Aware of the sovereignty of God, under the lordship of Jesus Christ and in the power and demonstration of the Holy Spirit, the miracles of Pierrepont will continue for whatever years are given to us. We look back with gratitude; we look up with wonder and faith; we look around with love and compassion; and we look forward with hope and expectancy.

*Rev. Jim Graham*
Pastor Emeritus
Gold Hill Baptist Church
January 2015

# About the Authors

*Jill Southern-Jones*
Jill Southern-Jones is the director of Ellel Ministries Pierrepont (Surrey, UK) and director of the NETS programme. She is known for her strong leadership, passionate Bible teaching and her pioneering spirit. She has taught in every continent in the world, except Antarctica, and travels regularly. When she is not travelling abroad, she can be found teaching on the NETS programme and at various Ellel Ministries' events in the UK. Jill is married to Colin who is also actively involved in the ministry at Ellel Pierrepont.

*Kathleen McAnear Smith*
Kathleen McAnear Smith completed NETS 20 and is an associate prayer minister at both Ellel Pierrepont and Ellel USA. Jill's reading of Ezekiel 34 during one of the teaching sessions at Pierrepont totally changed Kathleen's life, giving her a passion for sharing the healing message of Jesus for His disciples. Her two previous books, *Beyond Broken Families* (2011) and *Parents on the Move!* (2010) were published by Destiny Image Europe. Kathleen is married to Chris, also an associate prayer minister for Ellel Ministries, and between them they have six children and so far six grandchildren.

# About Ellel Ministries

## *Our vision*

Ellel Ministries is a non-denominational Christian mission organisation with a vision to resource and equip the Church by welcoming people, teaching them about the Kingdom of God and healing those in need (Luke 9:11).

## *Our mission*

Our mission is to fulfil the above vision throughout the world, as God opens the doors, in accordance with the Great Commission of Jesus and the calling of the Church to proclaim the Kingdom of God by preaching the good news, healing the brokenhearted and setting the captives free. We are, therefore, committed to evangelism, healing, deliverance, discipleship and training. The particular scriptures on which our mission is founded are Isaiah 61:1-7, Matthew 28:18-20, Luke 9:1-2,11, Ephesians 4:12, 2 Timothy 2:2.

## *Our basis of faith*

God is a Trinity. God the Father loves all people. God the Son, Jesus Christ, is Saviour and Healer, Lord and King. God the Holy Spirit indwells Christians and imparts the dynamic power by which they are enabled to continue Christ's ministry. The Bible is the divinely inspired authority in matters of faith, doctrine and conduct, and is the basis for teaching.

*For more information*

Please visit our website at www.ellelministries.org for full up-to-date information about the worldwide work of Ellel Ministries.

# ELLEL MINISTRIES CENTRES

**Ellel Grange (& International HQ)**
Bay Horse
Lancaster
Lancashire
LA2 0HN
Tel: 01524 751 651
Email: info.grange@ellelministries.org

**Ellel Glyndley Manor**
Stone Cross
Pevensey
East Sussex
BN24 5BS
Tel: 01323 440 440
Email: info.glyndley@ellelministries.org

**Ellel Pierrepont**
Frensham
Farnham
Surrey
GU10 3DL
Tel: 01252 794 060
Email: info.pierrepont@ellelministries.org

**Ellel Scotland**
Blairmore House
Glass,
Huntly
Aberdeenshire
AB54 4XH
Tel: 01466 799 102
Email: info.scotland@ellelministries.org

**Ellel Ministries Ireland**
Tel: +44 (0) 28 9260 7162 / 07545 696 750
Email: info.ireland@ellelministries.org

## Ellel Ministries Overseas Centres

**Ellel Ministries Africa**
PO Box 39569
Faerie Glen 0043
Pretoria
South Africa
Tel: +27 12 809 0031 / 1172
Email: info.africa@ellelministries.org

**Ellel Ministries Australia (Perth)**
PO Box 609
Northam 6401
Western Australia
Australia
Tel: +61 08 9622 5568
Email: info@wa.ellel.org.au

**Ellel Ministries Australia (Sydney)**
Gilbulla
710 Moreton Park Road
Menangle 2568
New South Wales
Australia
Tel: +61 02 4633 8102
Email: info.gilbulla@ellelministries.org

**Ellel Ministries Canada East**
183 Hanna Road
RR#2
Westport
Ontario, K0G 1X0
Canada
Tel: +1 613 273 8700
Email: info.emc@ellelministries.org

**Ellel Ministries Canada West**
Prairie Winds
31066 Range Road 20
Didsbury
Mountain View County
Alberta
T0M 0W0
Canada
Tel: +1 403 335 4900
Email: info.calgary@ellelministries.org

**Ellel Ministries France**
(Fraternite Chretienne)
10 Avenue Jules Ferry
38380 Saint Laurent du Pont
France
Tel: +33 47 65 54 266
Email: info.france@ellelministries.org

**Ellel Ministries Germany e.V.,**
Bahnhofstr. 45-47
72213 Altensteig
Germany
Tel: +49 7453 275 51
Email: buero@ellelgerman.de

**Ellel Ministries Hungary**
Veresegyhaz, PF17
2112, Hungary
Tel/Fax: +36 28 362 396
Email: info.hungary@ellelministries.org

**Ellel Ministries India**
502 Orchid Holy Cross Road
I. C. Colony
Borivili West
Mumbai
400103
India
Mob: +91 93 2224 5209
Email: info.india@ellelministries.org

**Ellel Ministries Malaysia – KL/Klang Valley**
9 & 11 Jalan Dendang 1
Kawasan 16
Berkeley Town Center
41300 Klang
Selangor D.E, Malaysia
Tel: +60 33 3599 011
Email: info.kl.malaysia@ellelministries.org

**Ellel Ministries Malaysia - Penang**
Lot 2-19, 7th floor, Harbour Trade Centre,
Gat Lebuh Macullum
10300 Penang
Malaysia
Tel: +60 12 4074 775 / +6012 410 9665
Email: info.penang.malaysia@ellelministries.org

**Ellel Ministries Malaysia - Sabah**
Lot 10 and 12, First Floor, Wisma Leven
Lorong Margosa 2, Luyang Phase 8,
88300 Kota Kinabalu,
Sabah, Malaysia
Tel: +60 88 265 800
Email: info.malaysia@ellelministries.org

**Ellel Ministries Netherlands**
Wichmondseweg 19
7223 LH Baak
The Netherlands
Tel: +31 575 441 452
Email: info.netherlands@ellelministries.org

**Ellel Ministries New Zealand**
PO Box 17690
Sumner
Christchurch 8840
New Zealand
Mob: +64 21 269 8384
Email: info.newzealand@ellelministries.org

**Ellel Ministries Norway**
Stiftelsen Ellel Ministries Norge
Grosas Centre
4724 Juevand
Norge
Tel: +47 6741 3150
Email: post@ellelnorge.no

**Ellel Papua New Guinea**
C/o Boroko Baptist Church
PO Box 1689
Boroko
National Capital District, 111,
Papua New Guinea
Tel: 675 7161 3587 / 675 767 33255
Email: info.png@ellelministries.org

**Ellel Romania**
Trotusului nr. 4
Oradea
410242
Bihor
Romania
Tel: +40 731 351 445
Email: contact@ellelromania.ro

**Ellel Ministries Rwanda**
P.O. Box 2964,
Kigali,
Rwanda

**Ellel Ministries Singapore**
39A Jalan Pemimpin
#05-01A
Halcyon Building
Singapore 577183
Tel: +65 6252 4234
Email: info@zion-ellel.org.sg

**Ellel Ministries Sweden**
Kvarnbackavagen 4 B
711 92 Vedevag
Sweden
Tel: +46 581 930 36
Email: info.sweden@ellelministries.org

**Ellel Ministries Switzerland**
Spitalweg 20
4125 Riehen
Switzerland
Tel: +41 61 645 42 17
Email: info.switzerland@ellelministries.org

**Ellel Ministries USA**
1708 English Acres Drive
Lithia
Florida 33547
USA
Tel: +1 813 737 4848
Email: info.usa@ellelministries.org

\* All details are correct at time of going to press February 2015 but are subject to change.
For up-to-date information about Ellel Ministries International please visit www.ellelministries.org

# Notes

## Chapter One: Let the Vision Begin!

1. We may need to be set free from the demons and their attack on our lives, but we are Christ's possession. In Ephesians 1:14 it talks about the Holy Spirit "who is a deposit guaranteeing our inheritance until the redemption of those who are God's possession – to the praise of his glory". We are God's possession.

2. Actually, at this time the ministry was just called Ellel Grange, as the other centres had not yet been purchased.

3. To learn more about Bill Subritsky, please see his website, www.doveministries.com (accessed 20.11.14).

4. Please see the Ellel Ministries website, www.ellel.org (accessed 20.11.14) for further details on Healing Retreats.

5. The Nine Week School is now called the Flagship Programme and runs at Ellel Grange, Lancashire, England. Course information can be found on the website, www.ellel.org/uk (accessed 20.11.14).

6. Please note that this was indeed a question from me and not ready compliance, as one must always check that the Holy Spirit directs and confirms a prophetic word.

## Chapter Two: Dealing with the Ploughing Equipment

1. I still don't know how either of us did this, and I give thanks for Ron's support.

2. Frensham is a village in the south of England, approximately an hour west of London. It is just a short drive outside a larger town called Farnham. Often Frensham is referred to as Farnham, for people who do not know the area. Our church was meeting just across the road from Pierrepont.

3. As an outstanding, mature Christian, Mrs Ione Carver was used to looking after pastors and people who would speak at church functions. She wanted her houseguest to have rest before leading a conference – quite understandable!

## Chapter Three: Three Good Reasons!

1. Jonny Wilkinson attended Pierrepont when it was a private school. Wilkinson was probably one of the world's most famous rugby players and in 2003 was named BBC Sports Personality of the Year.

## Chapter Four: Foundations

1. For a look at the history of the Billy Graham crusades, please see www.billygraham.org (accessed 20.11.14).

2. 'Just as I Am' is a hymn now in the public domain. It was written by Charlotte Elliott (1789–1871) and the music was by William B. Bradbury (1816–68).

3. The Navigators (www.navigators.org, accessed 20.11.14) are an evangelism and discipleship training organisation, equipping Christians for a life of faith through one-to-one relationships and small groups.

4. When you are a missionary, a 'furlough' is the term often used to refer to time you take off to go back home for the purpose of reconnecting with family and friends and speaking to your church sponsors.

5. Romans 11:29, "for God's gifts and his call are irrevocable" is a verse that gives me insight into what God was doing at this time.

6. A real estate term which means that if the borrower fails to make payments as agreed, the lender with a 'first charge' can repossess the property. Thus the property is in a 'first lien' position, taking priority over all other liens. In case of a foreclosure, the first mortgage will be repaid before any other mortgages.

7. The Boys' Covenanters was a Christian organisation for boys.

## Chapter Five: Every Knife, Fork and Spoon

1. Revelation 22:2.

2. From quite early on there were people totally dedicated, full-time, to establishing Pierrepont as an Ellel centre for Christian education and training. When someone "joined the team", they were counted as full-time employees, though often this meant not receiving a salary but having their basic living expenses covered. Volunteers often lived nearby, or within driving distance (many drove quite a distance) and worked when they were able.

3. Leviticus 18:27, 2 Chronicles 36:14, Isaiah 24:5, Ezekiel 37: 23, Matthew 23:25, 2 Corinthians 7:1.

4. Pierrepont house was listed in 1973 as a Grade II* listed building, which signifies its value to the history of England. Please see the English Heritage website, www.english-heritage.org.uk (accessed 21.11.14) for an explanation of the rating system. Having a listed building means an English Heritage historical officer has to agree to any alteration, even down to the type of paint used.

5. 2 Kings 2:19–21 Elisha threw salt, to represent cleaning and healing: "The men of the city said to Elisha, 'Look, our lord, this town is well situated, as you can see, but the water is bad and the land is unproductive.' 'Bring me a new bowl,' he said, 'and put salt in it.' So they brought it to him. Then he went out to the spring

and threw the salt into it, saying, 'This is what the LORD says: "I have healed this water. Never again will it cause death or make the land unproductive."'"

6. The Site and Facilities team does amazing restoration work and upkeep of the buildings and grounds at Pierrepont. This team is now called MSG (Maintenance, Sites and Grounds).

## Chapter Six: From Ministry of Defence to Ministry of Deliverance

1. Luke 4:16–20, Isaiah 61:1–2; see John 14:12.

2. Whitehall is a road in central London on which many UK government offices are based. Thus the term 'Whitehall' has come to mean the overall British government administration.

## Chapter Seven: No Turning Back

1. Bethany is a house on the Pierrepont site, used for several years by the Sites and Facilities team. It is now an administrative and accommodation building.

2. We are so thankful for the generosity of the Shell Trading & Shipping Company, 80 Strand, London for their donation of the blue tiles.

3. The work of Ellel Ministries in Scotland is based at Blairmore House – a beautifully restored Victorian country house about forty-five minutes north-west of Aberdeen.

4. *The Wind in the Willows* was based on a book of the same title by Kenneth Grahame. The movie was directed by Terry Jones and was produced in 1996.

5. Ian Coates later became deputy director of Ellel Grange for many years until he retired. Ian was a huge blessing to us at Pierrepont, as well as blessing many other people.

6. 'I Have Decided to Follow Jesus' is a hymn that originated in India. The lyrics are based on the last words of a man in north-east

India, who was called to renounce his faith by the village chief. He declared, "I have decided to follow Jesus." In response to threats to his family, he continued, "Though no one joins me, still I will follow." His wife was executed, and he was killed too, while singing, "The cross before me, the world behind me." His faith is reported to have led to the conversion of the chief and of other people who lived in the village. The Indian missionary Sadhu Sundar Singh (1889–1929) is credited with forming the man's words into a hymn. William Jensen Reynolds (1920–2009), an American hymn editor, composed an arrangement which became a regular feature of evangelist Billy Graham's meetings, hence its popularity.

## Chapter Eight: The Heart of God to the Heart of Man

1. See chapter two for the vision of the globe.

2. NETS is a unique programme for every Christian aged eighteen to eighty-plus who wants to be trained and equipped to follow their destiny in God and truly live the Christian life. On NETS you receive life-transforming training in healing, deliverance and discipleship. You embark on a journey that changes your life for the better and will greatly enhance your ministry.

3. Andy and Cath Taylor met at Ellel Grange, married and are raising three wonderful boys. Having worked at several Ellel centres, they went on to pioneer Ellel USA and Andy is now UK national director for Ellel Ministries.

4. Fiona Horrobin is Peter's wife, and an active leader in the work of Ellel Ministries. Fi, as she is affectionately called, is deeply involved in the development of much of the teaching, hard-won through many hours of prayer ministry to individuals.

5. Ezekiel 3:11, Matthew 25:21.

6. John and Paula Sandford started the Elijah House School of Ministry in 1975 and it is founded upon principles from Malachi 4:5–6 and Matthew 17:11. In the manner of Elijah, they call

THE MIRACLES OF PIERREPONT

God's people to restore the hearts of fathers to their children and the hearts of children to their fathers. They believe God is passionate to bring restoration to individuals, families, churches, communities, regions and nations. For further information check their website: www.elijahhouse.org (accessed 24.11.14).

## Chapter Nine: Prayer for Healing

1. Mrs Ione Carver was a naval officer's wife who had led a local young wives' group. She and her husband had held house parties where they and other couples spent the weekend seeking the Lord. Dr Stella Walter (she prefers "just Stella") was born in Afghanistan to medical missionary parents. Her father was killed by members of a tribe near to the clinic, but her mother returned with Stella to Afghanistan to serve for over thirty years. Stella did her medical training in London during the bombing of World War Two.

2. For more about healing through forgiveness, see Peter Horrobin's book *Forgiveness, God's Master Key*, published by Sovereign World Ltd. Log on to www.sovereignworld.com (accessed 25.11.14).

3. Matthew 6:14 is a good example, but there are hundreds of similar scriptural statements.

## Chapter Ten: Deliverance

1. 1 Peter 2:9, Ephesians 1:14, 1 Corinthians 6:19–20, 1 Corinthians 3:23, Ephesians 1:4–10 The Greek word used in the New Testament to describe a person with a demon (daimonizomai) does not mean 'to be possessed' but rather it means 'to have' a demon.

2. The Billy Graham Evangelism Association states: "After the Gospel has been preached and the stands have cleared ... after the stadium lights go out and the platform is dismantled ... does a

Crusade really make a difference in a community? A good work was begun in cities where evangelists Billy Graham, Franklin Graham and Ralph Bell have held Crusades. Now what?" Art Bailey, director of counselling and follow-up for Billy Graham Crusades, explains that "BGEA [Billy Graham Evangelistic Association] provides a team of local volunteers with a plan for organizing and training, as well as strategies for prayer, outreach and follow-up". He continues, "I think all Crusades are successful," he says. "But the local church – not BGEA – determines whether the Crusade will have a long term impact." www.billygraham.com

3. For much more on this subject, see the book *Healing Through Deliverance* by Peter Horrobin, published by Sovereign World www.sovereignworld.com (accessed 25.11.14).

4. If you look at chapter 34 of Ezekiel, you will see that God our Father is serious about rescuing and delivering His people! In Psalm 7:1 we see that we can call out for God's rescue. Other verses of note on this subject are: Isaiah 61:1, Matthew 6:13, Psalm 32:7, Joel 2:32, Philippians 1:19, 2 Corinthians 1:10.

## Chapter Twelve: Blessed are the Flexible!

1. At the beginning, we called the divisions of NETS 'Term One, Term Two' etc. Later these names were changed to 'Stage One, Stage Two' etc.

2. The minimum age for NETS is eighteen, and the oldest trainee so far was in her nineties.

3. Judy Miller was a team member at Pierrepont for many years, as well as making many visits to Africa with Flame International, bringing God's healing to communities suffering the effects of post-conflict trauma.

4. Matthew 5:16, 2 Thessalonians 1:3, 1 Thessalonians 5:11, Colossians 3:16.

5. Martin and Ginny Knapp later became directors of Ellel Grange until their retirement.

6. Clive Carr later helped to establish Ellel Ireland.

7. Trainees had general insurance, but it didn't cover them if the flight was booked before they got the visa. Because of the short timeframe we had between trainees arriving on Stage Three and committing to the mission trip, if we had waited until we got the visas, the flights would have cost several times more than they did. We learned from this experience and now we give trainees the choice – either that we book the cheaper flights, knowing that tickets will be non-refundable if they don't get a visa, or they get the visa first and we pray that cheap flights will still be available a few days before we leave. Generally we recommend waiting for the visa.

## Chapter Thirteen: You Are My Rock

1. Romans 11:29.

2. Ezekiel 11:19.